VEGAN PIZZA

OTHER BOOKS BY **JULIE HASSON**

Vegan Diner

150 Cupcake Recipes

The Complete Book of Pies

125 Best Cupcake Recipes

300 Best Chocolate Recipes

125 Best Chocolate Recipes

125 Best Chocolate Chip Recipes

VEGAN PIZZA

50 CHEESY, CRISPY, HEALTHY RECIPES

JULIE HASSON

**Andrews McMeel
Publishing, LLC**

Kansas City · Sydney · London

TO **JAY**, **SYDNEY**, AND **NOAH**—
YOU FILL MY LIFE WITH
SO MUCH LOVE!

Andrews McMeel Publishing, LLC
an Andrews McMeel Universal company
1130 Walnut Street, Kansas City, Missouri 64106

www.andrewsmcmeel.com

13 14 15 16 17 SDB 10 9 8 7 6 5 4 3 2 1

ISBN: 978-1-4494-2712-2

Library of Congress Control Number: 2013937456

Design: Diane Marsh

Photography: Ben Pieper, pages: ii, 5;
    all other photos courtesy of Istock.com

Digital/Photo Assistant: Anneka DeJong

Food Stylist: Trina Kahl

Food Stylist Assistant: Daniel Trefz

www.juliehasson.com

ATTENTION: SCHOOLS AND BUSINESSES
Andrews McMeel books are available at quantity discounts with bulk purchase for educational, business, or sales promotional use. For information, please e-mail the Andrews McMeel Special Sales Department: specialsales@amuniversal.com.

CONTENTS

ACKNOWLEDGMENTS

A million thank-you's to my incredible husband, Jay. You continue to make every day a fantastic adventure, and I know the best is yet to come. I love you madly!

A giant thank-you to my wonderful children, Sydney and Noah. I am so lucky to be your mom. And, Noah, thank you for eating pizza for dinner every night without a single complaint. Sydney, I'm so happy you could share in many of the pizza-making adventures, even when you were away at school. It was such fun to pack you up buckets of pizza dough to take back to school with you.

I also want to thank everyone involved with putting this book together. A giant thank-you to Lisa and Sally Ekus, for recommending me for this incredible project. It's always a pleasure working with you two. Another giant thank-you to Jean Lucas, my editor at Andrews McMeel, for making this book happen. I am extremely excited to be a part of this project! Thank you also to Diane Marsh, Dave Shaw, and Carol Coe.

Mom, thank you for sharing your love of delicious, healthy food with us. We learned firsthand through our backyard garden, the early-morning co-op buying trips to downtown LA, and loaf after loaf of your fresh-baked bread. To my always adorable brother, Jon—it's so much fun having two chefs in the family. We may live in different cities, but we share meals almost every day. Thank you, Dad and Ellen, for sharing my books with all of your clients. You may need to start building custom pizza ovens very soon.

A really big thank-you to Dan Butler, the man behind the magical Soy Curls; the awesome folks at Bob's Red Mill; and Madhava Natural Sweeteners. Your products are the best!

And, last but not least, thank-you to my wonderful crew of taste testers, who so enthusiastically baked and tested pizza recipes, always giving me your honest feedback: Kelly Cavalier, Sheree Britt, Kim Logan, Marti Miller-Hall, Jen Carlton Bailly, Danielle Aquilino, Rebekah Reid, Sara Goldstein, Matthew Bo, Dave Gibbons, and Cat DiStasio.

INTRODUCTION

Pizza has always been super close to my heart. When I was growing up, pizza was a special treat. We lived in Topanga Canyon, which is a rural area of LA, tucked away from civilization. At the time, it was a very long drive to the nearest pizza parlor, which was all the way out in Malibu. So it wasn't something that we got to do very often. But my brother and I knew that life was good if our parents packed us into our cherry red Volks-wagen hatchback to head out to Straw Hat Pizza. I can still remember the old movies playing on the wall, and big, frosty pitchers of root beer. Pizza was something special.

When my husband and I got married, we would throw big pizza parties in our backyard, with buckets of homemade dough and giant platters of toppings, all made to order and baked on top of our barbecue grill. Those parties were so much fun! Seriously, if you want to impress your guests, throw your home-made pizza dough on the grill and watch everyone ooh and aah.

Pizza making became our family tradi-tion. Yes, we could have easily gone to our local pizza joint and ordered pizza, but there is nothing like the homemade goodness of fresh pizza, made to order in your own kitchen or backyard. Once you've had home-made pizza, it's hard to eat pizza any other way, except maybe in Italy, but that's a whole other story.

As our kids got older, our pizza parties continued, whether for family dinners or birth-day parties, or whenever the mood struck. Our kids loved to jump in and help, kneading the dough, topping the pizzas with whatever veggies they were currently eating at the mo-ment, and customizing their creations accord-ing to their own personal tastes.

The pizza love went beyond our house too. I taught a lot of cooking classes in LA, with the pizza classes always filling up first. People seem to think that pizza is very labor-intensive to make at home, with hours of prep required. This couldn't be further from the truth! With a little planning, you can make the dough ahead of time and pull it out of the fridge in time for dinner.

Once I became vegan, I began to rethink and reconstruct my homemade pizzas. Instead of using dairy cheese, I made creamy vegan cheese sauces or used store-bought vegan cheese shreds, or I did without the cheese altogether and used a basil or sundried tomato pesto. Of course, the toppings are easy-peasy, with lots of fresh veggies, vibrant flavored spreads, and even vegan sausage, should you feel the need. Yes, you can find a large variety of vegan sausages and meats at most grocery stores these days. So all of the basic elements are still there: the crispy crust, the sauce, lots of toppings, and even the creamy cheese. Vegan pizza not only is delicious, but also happens to be a healthier choice, without the fat-laden cholesterol of the usual pizza pie.

I've created some super-easy pizza dough recipes, even for those that are fearful of yeast and the whole bread-making process. I have taken my tried-and-true dough recipe, the same one that I have been making for over twenty years, and made it almost foolproof. Thanks to the groundbreaking work of authors like Suzanne Dunaway, with her fabulous book *No Need to Knead*, and Zoë François and Jeff Hertzberg, with their extraordinary no-knead bread books, I was

able to take my tried-and-true pizza recipe, increase the water, and skip the kneading step. The results were absolutely stellar, better than ever, and the easiest dough that I've ever made. All you need is a bucket or a large bowl and a fork for mixing, and you're ready to go.

If you've been nervous about trying your hand at making dough, now is your chance to learn something new. Grab some flour, a bucket, and a fork, and go make yourself some pizza dough! This book is brimming with delicious recipes, from vibrant flavored pestos and spreads, meatless and wheat-less quinoa crumbles, and pizza combos like Chili Mac Pizza, Peanut Barbecue Pizza, and Eggplant Parmesan Pizza, to fresh vegetable–laden pizzas like Sweet Potato and Kale Pizza; Corn, Pesto, Zucchini, and Tomato Pizza; and Asparagus, Tomato, and Pesto Pizza. And let's not forget about dessert pizzas too, like Babka Pizza, Berry Pie Pizza, and Coconut-Caramel Pizza. So now you can create your own pizza traditions. Think pizza parties for summer entertaining, or "top your own" pizzas for your next dinner party. Have fun creating pizza masterpieces, right in your own kitchen. All of the ingredients that you will need to make your pizzas are in the pantry section. Then you'll be on your way to creating your own artisanal pizzas whenever the mood strikes.

THE PIZZA KITCHEN

PANTRY

Having a well-stocked pantry is a great way to be able to make pizza on the spot, whenever the mood might strike. It's perfect for busy weeknights when you want to make a delicious dinner, but don't want to spend the time running to the store for ingredients.

AGAVE SYRUP: Agave syrup is a natural sweetener made from the agave plant. Agave has a color, consistency, and taste similar to honey and comes in both light and amber. I really like Madhava and Wholesome Sweeteners brands of agave.

FLOUR: Look for specialty flours in well-stocked grocery or health food stores or online. I especially like the wonderful flours from Bob's Red Mill and Authentic Foods and used their flours for the recipes in this book. Note that there can be a difference in brands and types of flour, sometimes requiring recipes to need a touch more or less water. Weather can also play a role in this too. If it is cold, it may take longer for the dough to rise, and if it is dry, you may need to add more liquid or less flour.

BROWN RICE FLOUR: Brown rice flour is made by milling brown rice into flour. My two favorite brands are Bob's Red Mill and Authentic Foods.

FINE CORNMEAL: Fine-grind cornmeal is stone ground from whole yellow corn. I prefer the fine grind in the gluten-free dough, as it contributes to a better texture.

SORGHUM FLOUR: Sorghum is a millet-like cereal grain, which is ground or milled into a soft, fine, gluten-free flour. It is a powerhouse of nutrition, and adds a superb flavor to

gluten-free baking. My favorite is the "sweet" white sorghum flour from Bob's Red Mill.

SWEET RICE FLOUR: Sweet white rice flour is made from high-starch, short-grain rice and is very different from regular rice flour. Please note that sweet rice flour is definitely not interchangeable with regular rice flour. Sweet rice flour is what binds everything together in the quinoa crumble recipes, so it is vital that it sticks everything together perfectly, without allowing the crumbles to fall apart or become too gluey. There can be a big difference between brands of sweet rice flour. The two brands that I have found to work best in the quinoa crumble recipes are Bob's Red Mill and Authentic Foods. If you use another brand, you may need to add less of it to the recipe, depending on the brand. I found that the packages of sweet rice flour from Asian markets worked the worst in the recipes. Mochiko Sweet Rice Flour will work, but seems to be a somewhat stronger flour, so start with 3 to 4 tablespoons in the recipe, and add more as needed.

TAPIOCA STARCH/FLOUR: Tapioca starch is a starch extracted from the cassava root and is completely gluten-free. Take note, though, that not all brands of tapioca starch are created equal. I find that some brands of tapioca starch can have an off flavor, and that some vary in their absorption capabilities. My favorite go-to brands of tapioca starch are Authentic Foods and Shiloh Farms.

UNBLEACHED ALL-PURPOSE FLOUR: Unbleached all purpose flour is milled or ground from wheat berries. I prefer the unbleached, as it is never chemically bleached or bromated.

WHITE RICE FLOUR: White rice flour is made by milling white rice. I like to use white rice flour in my gluten-free crust, as it makes the crust crispier.

WHITE (OR LIGHT) SPELT FLOUR: White spelt flour is made by grinding whole spelt grains into flour and then removing most of the bran and germ.

WHITE WHEAT FLOUR: White wheat flour is a whole wheat flour made from a new variety of hard wheat. It is stone ground, with a slightly sweet taste, light texture, and creamy color after baking. It's my favorite variety of whole wheat flour.

WHOLE GRAIN SPELT FLOUR: Spelt is an ancient variety of wheat, with a delicious nutty flavor. The flour is made by grinding whole spelt berries. It is not gluten-free.

WHOLE WHEAT FLOUR: This flour is made by grinding whole wheat berries. It has all of the nutritious bran and germ still intact.

GOCHUJANG: Gochujang is a Korean hot red pepper paste. It's not the same as Sriracha sauce and is actually a fermented chili paste, made from glutinous rice powder mixed with powdered fermented soybeans and red peppers. The flavor is very deep and complex, and I highly recommend searching this paste out. The flavors will amaze you. You can find it at Asian markets and grocery stores, and online.

INSTANT YEAST: Instant yeast makes pizza crusts almost foolproof. I particularly like the SAF brand, as well as Red Star Quick-Rise Yeast (which are both manufactured by the same company). Instant yeast is very easy to use (no need to proof or pre-dissolve your yeast). It's also fast-acting and very reliable, even for beginners. Look for instant yeast in inexpensive 1-pound packages in club stores, restaurant supply stores like Cash and Carry and Smart and Final, or online stores such as King Arthur Flour. Keep your yeast in the freezer in an airtight container for a year or more (allow it to come to room temperature before using). Instant yeast is sometimes sold or labeled as quick yeast, rapid-rise active dry yeast, or fast-rising or fast-acting dry yeast. Make sure to not let the dry yeast come into direct contact with salt or sugar. Mix your flour, salt, sugar, etc., together first and then add your yeast.

LIQUID SMOKE: Liquid smoke adds a wonderfully smoky flavor to recipes. It is in fact vegan and natural, although check the ingredients label because some varieties add unnecessary ingredients.

NUTRITIONAL YEAST FLAKES: Dried flakes derived from yeast are high in B vitamins, protein, and minerals. Nutritional yeast also acts as a flavor enhancer in food. I especially love Red Star brand nutritional yeast flakes, which have a great flavor. They will last a long time if stored in an airtight container in a cool, dark place. I store mine in the pantry.

QUINOA: Quinoa is an ancient grain that is quick cooking, is a complete protein, and is packed with vitamins and minerals. It has a natural, bitter coating that needs to be rinsed off before cooking. Some brands, like Bob's Red Mill, have already removed it before packaging. I like to use quinoa in combination with textured vegetable protein (TVP) or textured soy protein (TSP) for Quinoa Crumbles.

SALT: All of the recipes in this book were tested with fine sea salt.

SMOKED PAPRIKA: Smoked paprika is also known as *pimentón* or Spanish paprika. When used in cooking, it imparts a fantastic smoky flavor to food.

SOY CURLS: Soy curls are a delicious and versatile product made from whole, non-GMO soybeans. These come in dried strips and simply need to be reconstituted in hot broth or water for 10 minutes. They are available online and in some health food stores.

SUGAR: Not all sugars are vegan, as cane sugar is sometimes filtered through bone char (from animals). Organic sugar, also sometimes labeled as evaporated cane juice, is processed without the use of bone char. I prefer to use organic sugar.

TAHINI: Tahini is hulled and toasted sesame seeds that have been ground into a paste. It's rich in calcium and protein, with a creamy and nutty flavor.

TAMARI: I love tamari's rich and savory flavor. It adds a little umami, or meaty savoriness, to a recipe, whenever you need a deeper flavor. You can substitute regular or low-sodium soy sauce for the tamari in all of the recipes in this book. If you can't find low-sodium tamari, which is what I prefer, you can add a little water to your tamari, mixing two-thirds tamari with one-third water, or even up to one-half tamari and one-half water. The version with water may not last as long, so I suggest refrigerating it and using it within a couple of weeks.

TVP OR TSP: Textured vegetable protein (TVP) and textured soy protein (TSP) are both essentially the same thing. They're made from defatted soy flour, which is low in fat, high in protein, and cooks quickly. There is also an organic TSP that can be used, which sometimes requires a little less hot water to rehydrate than the non-organic version. If it seems too wet, simply sprinkle in a little more of the dry TSP to absorb the rest of the water.

VEGAN SOUR CREAM: There are a couple of brands of vegan, non-dairy sour cream on the market. My first choice is Tofutti, which is what I used for testing the recipes in this book.

XANTHAN GUM: Xanthan gum is used to add volume and viscosity to gluten-free bread and baked goods.

EQUIPMENT

In the grand world of pizza baking, there are a few kitchen tools and equipment that will not only help make your life easier, but also make pizza prep a snap. Drawing on my experience in professional kitchens (and my love of kitchen gadgets), this is a list of equipment that will turn your kitchen into a mini vegan pizzeria.

BLENDER: This really helps in a vegan kitchen, from blending cashews into a silken cream to whipping silken tofu into a luscious mousse. There are two brands that I use and love: the infamous Vitamix and the Blendtec Total Blender models. Power and wattage do make a huge difference when it comes to a blender, as the stronger the motor, the better job it does blending your ingredients. Both Vitamix and Blendtec can blend cashews and water into a super-creamy milk, without a trace of grittiness from the nuts.

CAMBRO BUCKETS: Cambro buckets are food-safe containers with a tight-fitting lid that are absolutely perfect for mixing and storing your dough. The 4- and 6-quart sizes are very versatile and will hold a regular batch of dough, plus allow room for rising. The 6-quart size will probably hold the large batch of dough as well (but you may not want to put the lid on too tight, to allow room for the gases that build up). I usually just use an 8-quart bucket for the double batch of dough, although the bucket may not fit in most refrigerators. For the gluten-free dough, a 4-quart size works great. These buckets are under $10, and you can find them at local restaurant supply stores or online, such as at Amazon.com or King Arthur Flour. The other thing that I love about Cambro buckets is that they have markings on them, so you can visually see how much the dough has risen.

CAST-IRON PIZZA PAN: I love the Lodge Pro Logic cast-iron 14-inch pizza pan, which produces a nice crisp crust, much like pizzas baked on a pizza stone. No greasing necessary, and the size gives you some flexibility with the size pizza you want to bake.

DIGITAL KITCHEN SCALE: This is truly the most accurate way to bake, especially when you want consistent results every time. I have included ingredient weights for the dough recipes in this book, so that your dough will always come out perfectly. Digital scales also make baking and cooking easier and faster, since you can keep measuring the ingredients into the same bowl, zeroing it out each time. Look for digital scales with a tare function that measures in both grams and ounces. Find them in well-stocked kitchen stores and online. There are many excellent brands to choose from. My kitchen scale is an Escali, which I have been using daily for the past seven years.

INSTANT-READ THERMOMETER: If you don't already have one of these important baking tools in your cabinet, I suggest you run out and pick one up. They are relatively inexpensive. When you are making yeasted dough, it is imperative not to use water that is too hot, or else you can kill the yeast. This tool will prevent that from ever happening. Look for these thermometers in kitchen stores, restaurant supply stores, and online.

LIQUID MEASURING CUPS: The most accurate way to measure liquid ingredients is in glass or plastic liquid measuring cups with a lip or spout. I like to keep a variety of different sizes in my kitchen for baking.

METAL DRY MEASURING CUPS: With the exception of a digital scale, this is the most accurate way to measure dry ingredients, and the way that I measure my flour if I'm not using a digital scale. Always spoon your flour or other dry ingredients into the cup and level the top by scraping across with the flat side of a knife (or skewer). This will give you an accurate measurement.

METAL MEASURING SPOONS: This is the most accurate way to measure small amounts of both liquid and dry ingredients, if you're not using a scale.

OVEN THERMOMETER: If your oven temperature seems wonky, grab yourself an oven thermometer. It will let you know where your oven is at, and if you need to make any adjustments to the temperature setting.

PIZZA PEEL: When I first bought a pizza peel, I wondered how often I would use it. Wow, was I surprised, as I found it enormously useful! Once my dough is rolled out, I like to put it on a piece of parchment paper and slide it onto a pizza peel. That way it's super simple to slide it onto the hot pizza stone. If you don't have a peel, you can flip a baking sheet upside down and use it as you would a peel. Well, sort of. Pizza peels are often under $20.

PIZZA STONE: You can find pizza stones at most kitchen or club stores these days. I have a run-of-the-mill stone, which I preheat at the same time that I'm preheating my oven. Pizza comes out so much crispier on a preheated stone, which in my book makes it worth the $15 to $30 price tag.

ROLLING PIN: You can shape your pizzas by hand, by either hand-stretching or twirling the dough, or roll it out with a rolling pin. If you choose a rolling pin, I highly suggest using a silicone one, either a little one that fits in your hand or a large, heavy one. You can find them in specialty kitchen shops or online, such as at Amazon.com.

SILICONE ROLLING MAT: This is an incredibly useful and awesome tool for rolling out dough. The mat that I used is a Silpat Roul'Pat, which is made by the same company that makes Silpat silicone baking-sheet liners (which can also be used in a pinch too). I recommend checking these out, since you can use less flour to roll your dough, which results in a better textured crust. The Roul'Pat also works really well for pie dough too.

TIPS AND TRICKS

- Read the entire recipe through before starting. This way you know both the steps and the ingredients in the recipe before you start.

- Make sure that your oven is properly preheated before baking. It will probably take between 15 and 20 minutes to preheat, depending on your oven. All of the pizzas in this book are best baked in a preheated 500°F oven. Don't worry if your oven only goes to 450°F. It will still work, although it might take the pizza a few minutes longer to bake.

- When measuring dry ingredients, try to weigh out all of your ingredients. If you don't have a digital scale, then spoon your dry ingredients into dry measuring cups or spoons, and level the tops by scraping across with the flat side of a knife (or skewer).

- If you don't have a thermometer to check the temperature of your water, make sure to use warm tap water. Never microwave or boil your water first, as it's sure to get the water too hot. If the water is too hot (you never want it over 130°F), it will kill your yeast.

- **KNOW YOUR DOUGH:** This is not your *nona*'s pizza dough. This is a very wet dough, which you may be tempted to add a bunch of flour to, to firm it up, but please don't. The wet dough has so much flavor, and adding too much flour will change it. So this is what you want to do: Start with a little flour on your work surface (maybe a couple of tablespoons or so to begin with, dusted over the surface). Oh, and if you happen to have a silicone Silpat or Roul'Pat mat, use it here! If you have a scale, weigh your dough out. The Easy-Peasy Pizza Dough (page 2) should weigh 179 grams, or 6¼ ounces, for a small pizza and 359 grams, or 12½ ounces, for a large. Lightly dust your dough with flour on both sides, and stretch or roll it out into 1 large or 2 small rounds, as thinly as you can get it. Sprinkle with additional flour if you need it. I like to make my small pizzas about 11 inches and the large between 14 and 15 inches. Don't worry if your dough tears. Simply patch it back together with your fingers. Lightly dust with additional flour if your dough is too sticky.

- You can use the gluten-free dough for most, if not all, of the pizza recipes in this book. Just remember to make thin-crusted individual pizzas with it.

- **HOST A PIZZA PARTY!** Pizza parties are one of my favorite ways to entertain. Make up a big batch of dough several days ahead of time and keep it in your fridge. Then all you have to do is prep the toppings and you're good to go. Have a fun variety of fresh toppings, like vegan cheese, pesto, tomato sauce, olives, sliced bell peppers, finely sliced onions, and mushrooms. Roll or shape small pizzas, and place them on parchment paper rounds. Use pieces of cardboard, paper plates (if the pizzas are small enough), or thin cutting boards as makeshift pizza peels (for support when transporting them to the oven). Write everyone's name on the parchment, and let your guests garnish with their choice of toppings. Either bake the pizzas in the oven or on a preheated barbecue grill (with a closable lid to simulate an oven).

- **USE WHAT YOU'VE GOT:** Off-the-cuff pizzas are awesome! If what you've got in your fridge is a green bell pepper, an onion, and some barbecue sauce (along with some rising or refrigerated dough), then you're set. There is no one proper way to make a pizza. Experiment with flavors, use what you've got, and, most of all, have fun. Is there really ever a bad homemade pizza? I think not.

- **CREATE YOUR OWN MASTERPIECE PIZZAS:** Think of the recipes in this book as a delicious starting point or launchpad to your new vegan pizza–making career. I've given you the base recipes (crusts, sauces, and faux meats), from which you can continue building. Just think of the bounty of incredible vegetables at your local farmers' market, which is a perfect place to start. Love wild mushrooms? Create a mushroom lover's pizza, complete with a finish of truffle salt and truffle oil. Have a hankering for broccoli rabe or roasted butternut squash pizza? Make yourself one. Do you fancy fresh summer peaches or apricots? Top a baked pizza crust with a swirl of lightly sweetened vegan cream cheese or sour cream (with a hint of almond extract, lemon zest, or the seeds from a vanilla bean). Top with slices of fresh apricots or peaches (or luscious summer berries), and you have an amazing dessert.

- **GET CHEESY:** Vegan cheese can be a dream come true, but there are a couple of things that I have learned along the way. Number one: Less is more. A little vegan cheese goes a long way. I think that a fantastic vegan pizza is not about how much cheese you can top it with, but about using just enough to add a nice creaminess to your pie. And, hey, if you decide that you still want more cheese on your pizza, go for it. Number two: I found that vegan cheese (especially the Daiya brand) melts best if layered right on top of the sauce and under all of the fresh vegetables and toppings. You want the cheese to be nice and melty, not crisp and browned.

- If you have extra pizza dough on your hands, make breadsticks or sandwich rolls. For breadsticks, simply roll the dough on a well-floured surface into thin sticks (remember rolling clay into stick shapes for pinch pots in grade school? Just like that!). Place the unbaked breadsticks on a parchment paper–lined baking sheet and bake in a preheated 450°F oven until golden brown. You can also brush the unbaked breadsticks with a little olive oil and sprinkle them with a variety of seeds and coarse salt. To make rolls, shape the dough into sandwich-size rolls or buns on a well-floured surface, place the shaped rolls on a parchment paper–lined baking sheet, cover with a towel for 30 minutes to let rise slightly, and bake in a preheated 450°F oven until nicely golden brown and crisp on the outside.

- **MOST OF ALL, HAVE FUN!**

DOUGH AND CRUSTS

1

This dough is one that I have been making for about twenty years, and it always comes out perfect. The only change that I've made is, instead of kneading it like I used to do, I was inspired by the no-knead method in *Artisan Bread in Five Minutes a Day*, by Jeff Hertzberg and Zoë François, and now simply stir the ingredients together. The dough is delicious and flavorful and is super easy to make. Plus, no mixer required! The dough will keep in the refrigerator for up to 5 days, so you can make the dough ahead of time, and bake-off a quick and delicious pizza for dinner.

EASY-PEASY PIZZA DOUGH

Makes **2 large** (14- to 15-inch) or **4 individual** (about 11-inch) thin-crust pizzas

3 cups (408 grams) unbleached all-purpose flour

1 teaspoon (6 grams) fine sea salt

2 teaspoons (7 grams) instant yeast, at room temperature

1¼ cups (277 grams) warm water (110° to 120°F)

2 tablespoons (20 grams) extra virgin olive oil

2 tablespoons (32 grams) agave syrup, or 2 tablespoons (24 grams) light brown sugar, packed

1 In a large bowl or a food-safe 4-quart plastic Cambro bucket, combine the flour and salt, mixing well with a fork. Sprinkle the yeast on top of the dry mixture, and add the warm water, olive oil, and agave or sugar, and stir with a fork until everything is combined well and there are no traces of flour left. If the dough seems dry, add a little more water as necessary to make a soft, moist dough. There is no need to knead this dough.

2 Cover the bowl or bucket with plastic wrap or a fitted lid, and set aside in a warm place to rise for 2 to 3 hours (or up to 6 hours). At this point, you can also refrigerate it, covered, for up to 5 days, or divide the dough into 2 or 4 pieces and freeze them in a sealed zip-top bag (with room for dough expansion) for up to 2 weeks. Thaw the frozen dough overnight in the refrigerator before shaping.

3 Shape and bake the pizza according to the recipe directions.

VARIATION: For even more flavorful dough, reduce the yeast to ½ teaspoon, and let rise for about 18 hours before using or refrigerating to use at a later time. Don't do this with the gluten-free dough.

TIP: If you don't have a thermometer, make sure that your water isn't too hot. It should be warm water from the tap, not heated in the microwave or boiled. If the water is too hot, it can kill the yeast.

SIDEBAR

After making many, many batches of pizza dough, I started thinking about a trick that bakeries often use. They take a piece of the previous dough (about 3 ounces or so), and add it to the new dough, which infuses a lot of flavor. I gave it a try and it worked beautifully. Just make sure to stir the dough into the hot water first, so that you can break it up and it will mix into the new dough more easily. Then add the rest of your wet and dry ingredients, stirring until it's well mixed. I have been doing this for a while now, and I can only imagine how flavorful it will continue to get. Remember that the dough won't keep longer than about 5 days, so if you want to keep this going, you'll need to make a new batch of pizza dough every week or so (or freeze your piece of dough for up to 1 month).

Pizzas make fabulous party food, whether you're making tiny ones for appetizers, individual pizzas, or even pizzas on the barbecue. So when you've got a group coming over, make up this large batch of dough, which you can start much earlier in the day.

PIZZA DOUGH FOR **A CROWD**

Makes **4 large** (14- to 15-inch) or **8 individual** (about 11-inch) thin-crust pizzas

6 cups (816 grams) unbleached all-purpose flour

2 teaspoons (12 grams) fine sea salt

2 teaspoons (7 grams) instant yeast, at room temperature

2½ cups (554 grams) warm water (110° to 120°F)

¼ cup (40 grams) extra virgin olive oil

¼ cup (64 grams) agave syrup, or ¼ cup (48 grams) light brown sugar, packed

1 In a very large bowl or a food-safe 6- or 8-quart plastic Cambro bucket, combine the flour and salt, mixing well with a fork. Sprinkle the yeast on top of the dry mixture, and add the warm water, olive oil, and agave or sugar, and stir with a fork until everything is combined well and there are no traces of flour left. If the dough seems dry, add a little more water as necessary to make a soft, moist dough. There is no need to knead this dough.

2 Cover the bowl or bucket with plastic wrap or a fitted lid, and set aside in a warm place to rise for 2 to 3 hours (or up to 6 hours). At this point, you can also refrigerate it, covered, for up to 5 days, or divide the dough into 4 or 8 pieces and freeze them in a sealed zip-top bag (with room for dough expansion) for up to 2 weeks. Thaw the frozen dough overnight in the refrigerator before shaping.

3 Shape and bake the pizza according to the recipe directions.

TIP: For a personal-size pizza, each ball of dough should weigh about 179 grams or 6¼ ounces, and a large pizza 359 grams or 1½ ounces.

White wheat adds a delicious and nutty flavor, as well as added nutrition, to your pizza crust. You can play around with the percentages of wheat flour, adding more or less depending on your taste. I love this dough, and my son happily eats it without asking if it's whole wheat (the ultimate test)!

WHITE WHOLE WHEAT PIZZA DOUGH

Makes **2 large** (14- to 15-inch) or **4 individual** (about 11-inch) thin-crust pizzas

2 cups (259 grams) white wheat flour

1 cup (133 grams) unbleached all-purpose flour

1 teaspoon (6 grams) fine sea salt

2 tablespoons (24 grams) packed brown sugar

2 teaspoons (7 grams) instant yeast, at room temperature

1¼ cups (277 grams) warm water (110° to 120°F)

2 tablespoons (20 grams) extra virgin olive oil

1 In a large bowl or a food-safe 4-quart plastic Cambro bucket, combine the flours, salt, and brown sugar, mixing well with a fork. Sprinkle the yeast on top of the dry mixture, and add the warm water and olive oil, and stir with the fork until everything is combined well and there are no traces of flour left. If the dough seems dry, add a little more water as necessary to make a soft, moist dough. There is no need to knead this dough.

2 Cover the bowl or bucket with plastic wrap or a fitted lid, and set aside in a warm place to rise for 2 to 3 hours (or up to 6 hours). At this point, you can also refrigerate it, covered, for up to 5 days, or divide the dough into 2 or 4 pieces and freeze them in a sealed zip-top bag (with room for dough expansion) for up to 2 weeks. Thaw the frozen dough overnight in the refrigerator before shaping.

3 Shape and bake the pizza according to the recipe directions.

VARIATION: If you can't find white wheat flour, you can substitute regular whole wheat flour, which will give the dough a slightly more pronounced whole wheat flavor and darker color.

Spelt is actually a distant cousin of domestic wheat, with a lovely, nutty flavor. Although spelt flour does contain gluten, it contains less, which makes it easier for some people to eat who are sensitive to wheat.

SPELT DOUGH

Makes **2 large** (12- to 14-inch) or **4 individual** (8- to 9-inch) thin-crust pizzas

3¼ cups (383 grams) white spelt flour

1 teaspoon (6 grams) fine sea salt

2 teaspoons (7 grams) instant yeast, at room temperature

1¼ cups (277 grams) warm water (110° to 120°F)

2 tablespoons (20 grams) extra virgin olive oil

2 tablespoons (32 grams) agave syrup

1 In a large bowl or a food-safe 4-quart plastic Cambro bucket, combine the flour and salt, mixing well with a fork. Sprinkle the yeast on top of the dry mixture, and add the warm water, olive oil, and agave, and stir with the fork until everything is combined well and there are no traces of flour left. If the dough seems dry, add a little more water as necessary to make a soft, moist dough. If the dough is super wet, you can stir in a little more flour. Remember that this is a wetter dough. There is no need to knead this mixture.

2 Cover the bowl or bucket with plastic wrap or a fitted lid, and set aside in a warm place to rise for 2 to 3 hours (or up to 6 hours). At this point, you can also refrigerate it, covered, for up to 5 days, or divide the dough into 2 or 4 pieces and freeze them in a sealed zip-top bag (with room for dough expansion) for up to 2 weeks. Thaw the frozen dough overnight in the refrigerator before shaping.

3 Shape and bake the pizza according to the recipe directions.

VARIATION: Use half whole grain spelt flour and half white spelt flour for a stronger whole grain flavor and color. Sometimes whole grain spelt flour may need a touch more or less water. The dough should be very moist and soft.

If you're looking for a crisp, chewy, thin-crust gluten-free pizza, then this is your recipe. Part of the magic herein lies with the hard apple cider or gluten-free beer, which not only creates a nice chemistry with the yeast, but also adds a really lovely depth of flavor to this crust. This recipe was inspired by a gluten-free crust from the fabulous bread-baking duo of Zoë François and Jeff Hertzberg.

GLUTEN-FREE
PIZZA DOUGH

Makes **4 individual** (9-inch) thin-crust pizzas

1½ cups plus 2 tablespoons (239 grams) white rice flour

¼ cup (30 grams) brown rice flour

⅓ cup (38 grams) tapioca flour/starch

⅓ cup (54 grams) fine yellow cornmeal

2 tablespoons (23 grams) granulated sugar

1 teaspoon (6 grams) fine sea salt

1 teaspoon (3 grams) xanthan gum

2 tablespoons (12 grams) golden flax meal

¼ cup (57 grams) boiling water

1 tablespoon (9 grams) instant yeast, at room temperature

½ cup (112 grams) warm water (110° to 120°F)

½ cup (112 grams) gluten-free hard apple cider (alcoholic, not juice) or gluten-free beer, at room temperature

2 tablespoons (20 grams) extra virgin olive oil

1 In a large bowl or a food-safe 4-quart plastic Cambro bucket, combine the white rice flour, brown rice flour, tapioca flour/starch, cornmeal, sugar, salt, and xanthan gum, mixing well.

2 In a cup or very small bowl, whisk together the flax meal and the boiling water. Make sure to mix it right away, or it can get lumpy. After about a minute or two, the mixture will become thick and viscous. Set aside to cool for a couple of minutes.

3 Sprinkle the yeast over the dry ingredients. Add the warm water, cider, and olive oil to the bowl or bucket, along with the flax mixture. Using a fork or wooden spoon, mix until the dough comes together and all of the flour is mixed in. Cover the bowl or bucket with plastic wrap or a fitted lid, and set in a warm spot to rise for 2 to 3 hours (or up to 5 hours), until doubled in size.

4 Bake as directed according to the recipe directions.

VARIATION: You can substitute sorghum flour for the white rice flour, although it will produce a softer crust.

TIPS: This dough needs to be shaped into individual thin crust pizzas. It doesn't work well as a large or thick-crusted pizza. Also, this dough is best used the same day that it's made. Extra dough can be baked as untopped flatbreads, which are delicious! You can use this dough for most, if not all, of the pizza recipes in this book. Just remember to make thin-crusted individual pizzas with it.

This recipe really works best with fine cornmeal. When you roll out your dough, use white rice flour, which will help give you the crispiest crust. This recipe can be doubled to make 8 individual pizzas.

Make sure that the hard cider doesn't contain honey, which would make it not vegan. Although a few brands do contain honey, most are naturally vegan.

Cornmeal adds a lovely buttery-tasting flavor to a pizza crust, as well as contributing a little extra crispiness. You can use this recipe interchangeably with Easy-Peasy Pizza Dough.

CORNMEAL DOUGH

Makes **2 large** (14- to 15-inch) or **4 individual** (about 11-inch) thin-crust pizzas

2 cups (285 grams) unbleached all-purpose flour

1 cup (146 grams) yellow cornmeal, preferably fine grind

1 teaspoon (6 grams) fine sea salt

2 teaspoons (7 grams) instant yeast, at room temperature

1¼ cups (277 grams) warm water (110° to 120°F)

¼ cup (40 grams) extra virgin olive oil

2 tablespoons (24 grams) granulated sugar

1 In a large bowl or a food-safe 4-quart plastic Cambro bucket, combine the flour, cornmeal, and salt, mixing well with a fork. Sprinkle the yeast on top of the dry mixture, and add the warm water, olive oil, and sugar, and stir with the fork until everything is combined well and there are no traces of flour left. If the dough seems dry, add a little more water as necessary to make a soft, moist dough. There is no need to knead this dough.

2 Cover the bowl or bucket with plastic wrap or a fitted lid, and set aside in a warm place to rise for 2 to 3 hours (or up to 6 hours). At this point, you can also refrigerate it, covered, for up to 5 days, or divide the dough into 2 or 4 pieces and freeze them in a sealed, zip-top bag (with room for dough expansion) for up to 2 weeks. Thaw the frozen dough overnight in the refrigerator before shaping.

3 Shape and bake the pizza according to the recipe directions.

BURGER Crumbles   14

PEPPERONI Crumbles   16

SAUSAGE Crumbles   18

TACO Crumbles   20

GARLIC Soy Curls   22

SWEET AND SMOKY Soy Curls   25

HOUSE-MADE MEATS

2

These burger crumbles are fabulous on Cheeseburger Pizza (page 72). Although I very rarely use packaged products, this is one occasion where the onion soup mix gives the crumbles a great savory flavor that you just can't get without it. If you want to make your own soup mix instead of store-bought, I've included a recipe in the sidebar.

BURGER CRUMBLES

Makes about **2 cups**

1 cup unflavored TVP (textured vegetable protein) or TSP (textured soy protein) granules

1 (1.1-ounce) package dry onion soup mix

½ teaspoon granulated garlic

¼ teaspoon smoked paprika

¼ teaspoon poultry seasoning

1 cup boiling water (if using organic TVP or TSP, reduce the boiling water to ¾ cup)

1 tablespoon reduced-sodium tamari or soy sauce

4 cloves garlic, finely minced or pressed

1 cup cooked and cooled quinoa

Freshly ground black pepper

5 tablespoons sweet rice flour

1 to 2 tablespoons olive oil

1 In a small to medium bowl, combine the TVP, soup mix, granulated garlic, smoked paprika, and poultry seasoning, mixing well. Add the boiling water, give it a quick stir to mix, and cover with a piece of foil. Let sit for 10 minutes.

2 Once the TVP is reconstituted, add the tamari, minced garlic, and quinoa to the TVP mixture, mixing well. Add a few grinds of black pepper. Sprinkle the sweet rice flour on top, and using your hands and a squeezing motion, mix the rice flour into the TVP until the mixture is thickened and somewhat sticky. You want to keep squeezing the mixture, so that it forms into clusters or crumbly bits and pieces.

3 Preheat a cast-iron skillet over medium-high heat, adding 1 to 2 tablespoons of the olive oil. Once the oil and skillet are hot, add the crumbles and cook for 5 to 10 minutes, until the crumbles are nicely browned and crispy in spots. Remove from the heat and set aside to cool, or use right away as a pizza topping. The crumbles will keep, refrigerated, for several days, in a covered container or sealed zip-top bag.

VARIATION: For a soy-free version, substitute an additional 1 cup of cooked quinoa for the TVP and water, and omit the tamari or soy sauce. Add salt to taste.

TIPS: Always check your labels to make sure that products are vegan, especially with products like soup mix. Sometimes companies change their formulas, and you don't have any idea unless you check the label.

If using organic TVP or TSP, reduce the boiling water to ¾ cup, as the organic variety usually requires less water.

SIDEBAR

If you can't find vegan onion soup mix locally or you would prefer to use a healthier, homemade option, here's a homemade version to try: In a bowl, mix together 2 tablespoons dried onion flakes, 1 tablespoon plus 1 teaspoon nutritional yeast flakes, 2 teaspoons dried parsley, 1 teaspoon granulated onion or onion powder, ½ teaspoon sea salt, and ½ teaspoon granulated sugar. Use the entire batch for a full recipe of burger crumbles. This mixture will store well, in a covered container, for several months, if you want to make several batches to use later on.

The inspiration for the pepperoni flavor comes from cookbook authors extraordinaire Joni Marie Newman and Celine Steen. The crumbles are not only healthier than real pepperoni (and meat-free) but super easy to make as well. Leftover crumbles are delicious tossed into other dishes, or even folded into a quesadilla (vegan, of course!).

PEPPERONI CRUMBLES

Makes about **2 cups**

1 cup unflavored TVP (textured vegetable protein) or TSP (textured soy protein) granules

1 tablespoon plus 1 teaspoon paprika

1 tablespoon plus 1 teaspoon granulated garlic

1 tablespoon nutritional yeast flakes

2 teaspoons smoked paprika

2 teaspoons granulated sugar

½ teaspoon fine sea salt, or to taste

1 cup boiling water (if using organic TVP or TSP, reduce the boiling water to ¾ cup)

2 tablespoons olive oil

1 to 2 tablespoons liquid smoke, depending on the strength of your liquid smoke

1 tablespoon tamari or soy sauce

4 cloves garlic, finely minced or pressed

1 cup cooked and cooled quinoa

Cayenne pepper

5 tablespoons sweet rice flour

1 In a small to medium bowl, combine the TVP, paprika, granulated garlic, nutritional yeast, smoked paprika, sugar, and salt, mixing well. Add the boiling water, give it a quick stir to mix, and cover with a piece of foil. Let sit for 10 minutes.

2 Once the TVP is reconstituted, add 1 tablespoon of the oil, the liquid smoke, tamari, garlic, and quinoa to the TVP mixture, mixing well. Add the cayenne pepper to taste. Sprinkle the sweet rice flour on top, and using your hands and a squeezing motion, mix the rice flour into the TVP until the mixture is thickened and somewhat sticky. You want to keep squeezing the mixture, so that it forms into clusters or crumbly bits and pieces.

3 Preheat a cast-iron skillet over medium-high heat, adding the remaining 1 tablespoon olive oil. Once the oil and skillet are hot, add the crumbles and cook for 5 to 10 minutes, until the crumbles are nicely browned and crispy in spots. Remove from the heat and set aside to cool, or use right away as a pizza topping.

VARIATION: For a soy-free version, substitute an additional 1 cup of cooked quinoa in place of the TVP and water, and omit the tamari or soy sauce. Add salt to taste.

TIP: This recipe can be halved. If making the pepperoni crumbles ahead of time, the flavor may not be quite as vibrant and strong the next day. Simply add a little more of the spices to liven them up again.

SIDEBAR

To cook quinoa, place 1½ cups of water in a large saucepan. Bring to a boil, and add 1 cup of rinsed and drained quinoa. Give it a stir, bring it to a simmer, reduce the heat to low, cover, and let cook for 15 minutes. Turn off the heat and let sit, covered, for another 5 minutes.

This is a fast and nutritious way to make sausage for your pizza. The homemade veggie meat has a lot of protein and flavor, which makes it perfect for topping your pizza, folding it into a calzone, or even tossing it into your favorite breakfast scramble.

SAUSAGE CRUMBLES

Makes about **2 cups**

1 cup unflavored TVP (textured vegetable protein) or TSP (textured soy protein) granules

1 tablespoon granulated onion

2 tablespoons nutritional yeast flakes

2 teaspoons paprika

2 teaspoons granulated garlic

1 teaspoon red chili flakes

½ teaspoon fine sea salt, or to taste

1 teaspoon fennel seeds

½ teaspoon dried oregano

1 cup boiling water (if using organic TVP or TSP, reduce the boiling water to ¾ cup)

1 tablespoon tamari or soy sauce

2 cloves garlic, finely minced or pressed

1 cup cooked and cooled quinoa

5 tablespoons sweet rice flour

1 to 2 tablespoons extra virgin olive oil

1 In a small to medium bowl, combine the TVP, granulated onion, nutritional yeast, paprika, granulated garlic, red chili flakes, salt, fennel seeds, and oregano, mixing well. Add the boiling water, give it a quick stir to mix, and cover with a piece of foil. Let sit for 10 minutes.

2 Once the TVP is reconstituted, add the tamari, minced garlic, and quinoa to the TVP mixture, mixing well. Sprinkle the sweet rice flour on top, and using your hands and a squeezing motion, mix the rice flour into the TVP until the mixture is thickened and somewhat sticky. You want to keep squeezing the mixture, so that it forms into clusters or crumbly bits and pieces.

3 Preheat a cast-iron skillet over medium-high heat, adding 1 to 2 tablespoons of the olive oil. Once the oil and skillet are hot, add the crumbles and cook for 5 to 10 minutes, until the crumbles are nicely browned and crispy in spots. Remove from the heat and set aside to cool, or use right away as a pizza topping.

VARIATION: For a soy-free version, substitute an additional cup of cooked quinoa for the TVP and water, and omit the tamari or soy sauce. Add salt to taste.

TIP: Look for organic TVP and TSP in your health food store and online. The organic TSP is a healthier choice and isn't processed with chemicals.

Taco crumbles are super easy to make and are fabulous layered on top of a pizza. One try, and you may forever change taco night to taco pizza night.

TACO CRUMBLES

Makes about **2 cups**

1 cup unflavored TVP (textured vegetable protein) or TSP (textured soy protein) granules

2 teaspoons granulated onion

2 teaspoons chili powder

2 teaspoons ground cumin

1 teaspoon granulated garlic

1 teaspoon dried oregano

½ teaspoon smoked paprika

½ teaspoon fine sea salt, or to taste

1 cup boiling water (if using organic TVP or TSP, reduce the boiling water to ¾ cup)

1 tablespoon tamari or soy sauce

2 to 4 cloves garlic, finely minced or pressed

1 cup cooked and cooled quinoa (see page 17)

5 tablespoons sweet rice flour

1 to 2 tablespoons olive oil

1 In a small to medium bowl, combine the TVP, onion, chili powder, cumin, granulated garlic, oregano, smoked paprika, and salt, mixing well. Add the boiling water, give it a quick stir to mix, and cover with a piece of foil. Let sit for 10 minutes.

2 Once the TVP is reconstituted, add the tamari, minced garlic, and quinoa to the TVP mixture, mixing well. Sprinkle the sweet rice flour on top, and using your hands and a squeezing motion, mix the rice flour into the TVP until the mixture is thickened and somewhat sticky. You want to keep squeezing the mixture, so that it forms into clusters or crumbly bits and pieces.

3 Preheat a cast-iron skillet over medium-high heat, adding 1 to 2 tablespoons of the olive oil. Once the oil and skillet are hot, add the crumbles and cook for 5 to 10 minutes, until the crumbles are nicely browned and crispy in spots. Remove from the heat and set aside to cool, or use right away as a pizza topping.

VARIATION: **For bolder-flavored taco crumbles, increase both the granulated onion and chili powder to 1 tablespoon. For a soy-free version, substitute an additional cup of cooked quinoa for the TVP and water, and omit the tamari or soy sauce. Add salt to taste.**

Soy Curls are a fabulous invention, as they come in dry strips and you only have to rehydrate and flavor them. These Garlic Soy Curls make a great topping for pizza, with a nice chewy texture and a great garlic flavor that will add pizzazz to your pies.

GARLIC SOY CURLS

Makes about **2 cups**

4 ounces Soy Curls

1½ cups boiling water

1 tablespoon tamari or soy sauce

1 teaspoon granulated garlic

Olive oil

2 tablespoons nutritional yeast flakes

Fine sea salt

1 In a small bowl, combine the Soy Curls and boiling water. Let stand until softened, about 10 minutes. Drain the Soy Curls, pressing out as much water as possible. You want them very dry.

2 Toss the Soy Curls with the tamari and granulated garlic.

3 Heat a large cast-iron skillet with 1 tablespoon of olive oil. Add the Soy Curls and cook, stirring often, until they are nicely browned, 10 to 15 minutes. The Soy Curls should have a nice chewy texture at this point. If necessary, drizzle in a little more olive oil as needed. Sprinkle the Soy Curls with the nutritional yeast flakes and give them a few stirs, until the Soy Curls are completely coated. Cook for another few minutes, until the nutritional yeast has begun to melt into them. Add salt to taste.

4 The Soy Curls are now ready to use on your pizza. Alternatively, let the cooked Soy Curls cool, and refrigerate until ready to use.

Sometimes you want just a little sweet and smoky flavor to play off the other flavors on your pizza. Well, this is it, and these Soy Curls are so good, you'll find yourself using them every chance you get. Leftover Sweet and Smoky Soy Curls will keep for several days, so you can make a batch ahead of time, and toss them on a pizza when the mood strikes. They are also lovely tossed in a salad, tucked into a sandwich, or just eaten out of hand.

SWEET AND SMOKY SOY CURLS

Makes about **2 cups**

4 ounces Soy Curls

1½ cups boiling water

1 tablespoon tamari or soy sauce

1 tablespoon liquid smoke

1 tablespoon maple syrup

1 tablespoon nutritional yeast flakes

1 teaspoon toasted sesame oil

½ teaspoon fine sea salt

Olive oil

continued on next page

TIP: **Soy Curls are great to keep on hand, as they are a dry product, and only need to be rehydrated before using.**

1 In a small bowl, combine the Soy Curls and boiling water. Let stand until softened, about 10 minutes. Drain the Soy Curls, pressing out as much water as possible. You want them very dry.

2 Toss the Soy Curls with the tamari, liquid smoke, maple syrup, nutritional yeast flakes, sesame oil, and salt.

3 Heat a large cast-iron skillet with 1 tablespoon of olive oil. Add the Soy Curls and cook, stirring often, until they are nicely browned, 10 to 15 minutes. The Soy Curls should have a nice chewy texture at this point. If necessary, drizzle in a little more olive oil as needed.

4 The Soy Curls are now ready to use on your pizza. Alternatively, let the cooked Soy Curls cool, and refrigerate until ready to use.

CHEDDARY CASHEW Cheese Sauce   28

CREAMY Cheese Sauce   29

SMOKY WHITE Cheese Sauce   30

SUN-DRIED TOMATO, BASIL, and **ARUGULA** Pesto   32

TOMATO-GARLIC Pizza Sauce   35

ZESTY Pesto   36

CHEESY SAUCES
AND SPREADS

3

Sometimes you just don't want to use a packaged cheese on your pizza, and that is where this silky cashew-based sauce comes in. It's creamy and delicious, and it can be whipped up in 15 minutes.

CHEDDARY CASHEW CHEESE SAUCE

Makes 1½ to 1¾ cups

½ cup raw unsalted cashews

¼ cup nutritional yeast flakes

1 teaspoon granulated onion

1 teaspoon smoked paprika

1 teaspoon fine sea salt

1 In the jar of a blender, combine 2 cups of water, the cashews, nutritional yeast, onion, smoked paprika, and salt.

2 Blend the mixture at high speed until completely smooth and no bits of nuts remain.

TIP: If you don't have a powerful blender, make sure to soak your cashews in water to cover for several hours. Drain the soaking liquid and proceed with the recipe. This recipe can be cut in half.

3 Pour the cashew mixture into a medium saucepan and bring to a simmer over medium heat, whisking continuously. Once the mixture comes to a simmer, lower the heat slightly and continue cooking and whisking until fairly thickened. This will take 10 to 15 minutes total. The sauce will continue to thicken as it cools. Use this sauce as directed in the recipe, or drizzle anywhere that you want a nice cheddary-flavored sauce, like over tacos or scrambles or tossed with cooked macaroni.

This sauce was created by the über-talented Chef Jeff Ridabock, at the Homegrown Smoker vegan barbecue food cart in Portland. It's fantastic on Chili Mac Pizza (page 74), and it can also be used interchangeably with Cheddary Cashew Cheese Sauce (page 28) in any of the recipes in this book. It's also nut-free.

CREAMY CHEESE SAUCE

Makes about 1¾ cups

1 cup plain unsweetened soy milk

¼ cup canola oil

2 ounces firm tofu (not silken)

1 cup nutritional yeast flakes

1 tablespoon low-sodium tamari

2 teaspoons granulated garlic

1 teaspoon paprika

1 teaspoon dry mustard

1 teaspoon salt

1 In a blender jar or the bowl of a food processor, combine the soy milk, oil, tofu, nutritional yeast, tamari, granulated garlic, paprika, dry mustard, and salt. Blend until super smooth and creamy.

2 Refrigerate the sauce in an airtight container until ready to use. This sauce will keep, refrigerated, for a day or two.

Even if you have access to a nice melty vegan cheese, there will still be times when nothing beats a homemade cheesy sauce. This sauce has a light smoky, savory flavor, which adds just the right creaminess to your pizza.

SMOKY WHITE CHEESE SAUCE

Makes about **2 cups**

½ **cup raw unsalted cashews**

¼ **cup nutritional yeast flakes**

2 **cloves garlic**

½ **teaspoon fine sea salt**

2 **tablespoons tahini**

½ **to 1 teaspoon liquid smoke**

1   In the jar of a blender, combine 2 cups of water, the cashews, nutritional yeast, garlic, salt, tahini, and liquid smoke.

2   Blend the mixture at high speed until completely smooth and no bits of nuts remain.

3   Pour the cashew mixture into a medium saucepan and bring to a simmer over medium to medium-high heat, whisking continuously. Lower the heat slightly to keep the sauce at a low simmer, and continue cooking and whisking until almost thickened. This will take about 10 minutes total. The trick is to cook the sauce on a fairly high heat so that it thickens quickly, but not hot enough to burn it. The sauce will continue to thicken as it cools. Use this sauce as directed in the recipe, or drizzle anywhere that you want a nice creamy, smoky-flavored sauce, like over scrambles or roasted or steamed vegetables, or tossed with cooked pasta.

VARIATION: For a less-smoky cheese sauce, reduce the liquid smoke to ¼ teaspoon.

TIP: If you don't have a strong, high-speed blender, make sure to soak your cashews in water to cover for several hours. Drain and proceed with the recipe.

This recipe is one from my catering days. I would toss pasta with this magnificent pesto, for a gorgeous summer salad. And, as good as this pesto is on pasta, it's even more fab on pizza!

SUN-DRIED TOMATO, BASIL, AND ARUGULA PESTO

Makes **1 generous cup**

¾ cup tightly packed fresh basil leaves (about 2¼ ounces)

1 ounce fresh arugula

⅓ cup sun-dried tomatoes, soft-dried, or oil-packed and drained

⅓ cup pitted Kalamata olives

½ cup raw walnuts

4 cloves garlic

2 tablespoons capers

¼ teaspoon fine sea salt

¼ cup extra virgin olive oil

1 In the bowl of a food processor, combine the basil, arugula, sun-dried tomatoes, olives, walnuts, garlic, and capers. Pulse to combine. Add the salt and oil, and pulse until lightly chunky. You don't want to make this a smooth pesto, as you want a little texture to it.

2 Spread the pesto on a baked or unbaked pizza crust, or refrigerate until ready to use. This sauce will keep, refrigerated, for several days.

VARIATION: You can add an extra handful of arugula for a slightly bolder (and greener-colored) pesto.

SIDEBAR

If you use the sun-dried tomatoes that come in a bag, which is what I usually use, look for a package where the tomatoes are soft and pliable. If they're not, simply cover with boiling water and soak until softened, 10 to 15 minutes. Drain and proceed with the recipe.

This is a lovely all-purpose red sauce, which works perfectly on most of the pizzas in this book. I like to make a batch and store it in a widemouthed 1-quart canning jar in my fridge, so that it's handy to grab whenever the urge hits to make a pizza. The sauce will last about 5 days refrigerated and can be frozen for longer storage, up to 1 month.

TOMATO-GARLIC
PIZZA SAUCE

Makes about 3½ cups

1 (28-ounce) can organic diced plum or San Marzano tomatoes (not drained)

3 to 4 large cloves garlic

1 teaspoon dried oregano

Salt

1 In the jar of a blender, combine the tomatoes, garlic, and oregano. Blend until smooth. Add salt to taste.

2 Use right away on a pizza, or refrigerate for longer storage.

VARIATION: For a richer sauce, add 1 to 2 tablespoons extra virgin olive oil and blend with the tomatoes. For a thicker-style tomato sauce, add one 6-ounce can tomato paste along with the canned tomatoes.

his really is the besto pesto. It will transform your pizzas from good to amazing. You can make this pesto ahead, as it will keep, refrigerated, for several days. This is also a much more healthful version, without the usual copious amounts of oil and cheese.

ZESTY PESTO

Makes about ¾ cup

4 ounces fresh basil leaves, washed and patted or spun dry

⅓ cup raw walnuts, raw pecans, or roasted skinned hazelnuts

4 cloves garlic

2 tablespoons nutritional yeast flakes

¼ teaspoon fine sea salt, plus more as needed

¼ cup extra virgin olive oil, plus more as needed

1 In the bowl of a food processor, combine the basil, walnuts, garlic, nutritional yeast, and salt. Pulse to combine. Add the oil and process until smooth. If the pesto mixture is too thick, add another tablespoon or two of oil as needed. Taste and adjust the salt as needed.

2 Use the pesto right away, or store in an airtight container in the refrigerator for several days.

TIP: If you have a salad spinner, it's the perfect tool for drying your basil after rinsing. I went and bought myself one after making up a batch of watery pesto. Let's just say the pesto tasted like water, and the subsequent batch made with the salad spinner was spectacular. Yay, kitchen gadgets!

SIDEBAR

Nutritional yeast adds a wonderful cheesiness to this pesto, allowing you to kick Parmesan to the curb. No cheese needed here.

THE CLASSICS

4

Sometimes you just want a good old-fashioned classic, served up pizzeria-style. Maybe it's the familiar flavors of sausage, cheese, and tomato sauce, or maybe it's the nostalgic feeling you get when tasting it. Whatever the case, this is a great crowd-pleaser pizza, as well as one that will satisfy you when you find yourself in the mood for something old school.

GARLIC, SAUSAGE, AND ONION PIZZA

Makes **1 large** (14- to 15-inch) pizza or **2 individual** (about 11-inch) thin-crust pizzas

1 batch pizza dough (see page 2)

½ cup Tomato-Garlic Pizza Sauce (page 35)

¾ to 1 cup shredded vegan mozzarella-style cheese

2 store-bought vegan sausages, thinly sliced, or Sausage Crumbles (page 18)

About ⅓ yellow onion, thinly sliced

2 cloves garlic, very thinly sliced

1 to 2 jalapeños, thinly sliced (optional)

1 Preheat the oven, preferably with a pizza stone inside, to 500°F for 30 minutes, while getting the pizza ready.

2 Divide your dough into 2 even pieces. Keep 1, and return 1 to the bucket, cover, and refrigerate for later use. On a lightly floured surface, stretch or roll out your dough into 1 large or 2 small rounds, as thin as you can get it. I like to make my small pizzas about 11 inches and my large between 14 and 15 inches. Don't worry if your dough tears. Simply patch it back together with your fingers. Lightly dust with additional flour if the dough is too sticky. Try not to use too much, or your crust will be very dry. Carefully transfer the rolled-out dough to a large sheet of parchment paper.

3 Spread the tomato sauce (about ¼ cup for each small pizza, and about ½ cup for a large) evenly on the pizza, leaving a ¼- to ½-inch border around the edge. Sprinkle the cheese over the sauce, and top with the sausage slices, onion, garlic, and jalapeño, if using. If making 2 small pizzas, repeat with the remaining pizza.

4 Carefully transfer the pizza with the parchment paper to the pizza stone, if using. Otherwise, place the pizza on a parchment-lined baking sheet, and place in the preheated oven. If making 2 small pizzas, repeat with the remaining pizza.

5 Bake for 10 to 15 minutes, until the cheese is melted and the crust looks fairly darkish brown. If it's not done, continue baking for a few more minutes.

6 Let the pizza cool for 5 minutes before cutting into slices, and serve right away.

I love that you can make vegan pizzas that are every bit as toothsome, flavorful, and meaty as traditional pizzas, without any animal products. This pizza reminds me of a meatball sub, and it had my son jumping for joy. It is often requested at our house, by both my husband and my son.

MEATBALL PIZZA

Makes **1 large** (12- to 13-inch) pizza

1 (28-ounce) can diced tomatoes, preferably organic

1 (6-ounce) can tomato paste

4 cloves garlic

1 (16-ounce) bag frozen veggie meatballs

1¼ teaspoons dried oregano

1¼ teaspoons dried basil

1 batch pizza dough (see page 2)

About ⅔ cup shredded vegan mozzarella-style cheese

¼ cup packed minced fresh parsley

1 Preheat the oven, preferably with a pizza stone inside, to 500°F for 30 minutes, while getting the pizza ready.

2 In a blender jar, combine the diced tomatoes, tomato paste, and garlic. Blend until smooth. Pour the tomato mixture into a large saucepan, and bring to a simmer over medium heat. You may want to cover the saucepan, as the tomato sauce has a tendency to spatter. Once the sauce is at a simmer, add the bag of frozen meatballs, plus the oregano and basil. Simmer the sauce for 10 to 15 minutes, until the meatballs are completely cooked through. Turn off the heat and set aside.

3 Divide your dough into 2 even pieces. Keep 1, and return 1 to the bucket, cover, and refrigerate for later use. On a lightly floured surface, stretch or roll out your dough into 1 large, 12- to 13-inch round. Don't worry if your dough tears. Simply patch it back together with your fingers. Lightly dust with additional flour if the dough is too sticky. Try not to use too much, or your crust will be very dry. Carefully transfer the rolled-out dough to a large sheet of parchment paper.

4 Carefully transfer the pizza and parchment paper to the pizza stone, if using. Otherwise, place the pizza on a baking sheet, and place in the preheated oven. Bake for 5 to 8 minutes, until the crust is golden. Carefully remove the pizza from the oven, and spread about ¾ cup of the meatball-and-sauce mixture evenly over the top for a small pizza or about 1½ cups or more for a large pizza, leaving a ¼-inch border around the edge. If the veggie meatballs are really large, you can cut them in half before spreading them on top of the pizza. Sprinkle the cheese over the sauce. Return the pizza to the oven and bake for another 5 minutes or so, until the cheese is melted. If it's not done, continue baking for a few more minutes.

5 Let the pizza cool for 5 minutes. Sprinkle the pizza with the minced parsley, cut into slices, and serve right away.

I mean "plain Jane" in the best possible way here. This is an unpretentious, classic pizza, with simple, traditional flavors: sauce, cheese, and pepperoni. Sometimes you just want to keep things simple.

PLAIN JANE PIZZA

Makes **1 large** (14- to 15-inch) pizza or **2 individual** (about 11-inch) thin-crust pizzas

1 batch pizza dough (see page 2)

½ cup Tomato-Garlic Pizza Sauce (page 35)

¾ to 1 cup shredded vegan mozzarella-style cheese

About 2 cups Pepperoni Crumbles (page 16) or store-bought vegan pepperoni slices

1 Preheat the oven, preferably with a pizza stone inside, to 500°F for 30 minutes while getting the pizza ready.

2 Divide your dough into 2 even pieces. Keep 1, and return 1 to the bucket, cover, and refrigerate for later use. On a lightly floured surface, stretch or roll out your dough into 1 large or 2 small rounds, as thin as you can get it. I like to make my small pizzas about 11 inches and my large between 14 and 15 inches. Don't worry if your dough tears. Simply patch it back together with your fingers. Lightly dust with additional flour if the dough is too sticky. Try not to use too much, or your crust will be very dry. Carefully transfer the rolled-out dough to a large sheet of parchment paper.

3 Spread the tomato sauce (about ¼ cup for each small pizza, and about ½ cup for a large) evenly on the pizza, leaving a ¼- to ½-inch border around the edge. Sprinkle the cheese over the sauce, and top with the pepperoni. If making 2 small pizzas, repeat with the remaining pizza.

4 Carefully transfer the pizza and parchment paper to the pizza stone, if using. Otherwise, place the pizza on a baking sheet, and place in the preheated oven. If making 2 small pizzas, repeat with the remaining pizza.

5 Bake for 10 to 15 minutes, until the cheese is melted and the crust looks fairly darkish brown. If it's not done, continue baking for a few more minutes.

6 Let the pizza cool for 5 minutes before cutting into slices, and serve right away.

This pizza reminds me a bit of a dish that my mom made when I was growing up called Joe's Special. There's just something about spinach, mushrooms, and onion that is so irresistibly good, and when combined with the homemade crumbles in this recipe, it's fantastic!

SPINACH, ONION, MUSHROOM, AND PEPPERONI PIZZA

Makes **1 large** (14- to 15-inch) pizza or **2 individual** (about 11 inch) thin-crust pizzas

1 batch pizza dough (see page 2)

½ cup Tomato-Garlic Pizza Sauce (page 35)

¾ to 1 cup shredded vegan mozzarella-style cheese

About 1½ ounces fresh baby spinach

About 1 cup sliced button or cremini mushrooms

About 2½ cups Pepperoni Crumbles (page 16)

About ⅓ red onion, thinly sliced

1 Preheat the oven, preferably with a pizza stone inside, to 500°F for 30 minutes, while getting the pizza ready.

2 Divide your dough into 2 even pieces. Keep 1, and return 1 to the bucket, cover, and refrigerate for later use. On a lightly floured surface, stretch or roll out your dough into 1 large or 2 small rounds, as thin as you can get it. I like to make my small pizzas about 11 inches and my large between 14 and 15 inches. Don't worry if your dough tears. Simply patch it back together with your fingers. Lightly dust with additional flour if the dough is too sticky. Try not to use too much, or your crust will be very dry. Carefully transfer the rolled-out dough to a large sheet of parchment paper.

3 Spread the tomato sauce (about ¼ cup for each small pizza, and about ½ cup for a large) evenly on the pizza, leaving a ¼- to ½-inch border around the edge. Sprinkle the cheese over the sauce, and top with an even layer of the spinach and mushrooms. Sprinkle an even layer of the Pepperoni Crumbles on top of the mushrooms and top with the onion slices. If making 2 small pizzas, repeat with the remaining pizza.

4 Carefully transfer the pizza and parchment paper to the pizza stone, if using. Otherwise, place the pizza on a baking sheet, and place in the preheated oven. If making 2 small pizzas, repeat with the remaining pizza.

5 Bake for 10 to 15 minutes, until the cheese is melted and the crust looks fairly darkish brown. If it's not done, continue baking for a few more minutes.

6 Let the pizza cool for 5 minutes before cutting into slices, and serve right away.

VARIATION: Substitute Burger Crumbles (page 14) or Sausage Crumbles (page 18) for the Pepperoni Crumbles.

Sometimes a simple, yet classic pizza is best, just like they do it in Italy. This is the holy trinity of Italian pizza, with the flavorful combination of fresh basil, ripe tomatoes, and creamy cheese. If you're really feeling daring, add some fresh sliced or chopped garlic on top.

TOMATO-BASIL PIZZA

Makes **1 large** (14- to 15-inch) or **2 individual** (about 11-inch) thin-crust pizzas

1 batch pizza dough (see page 2)

½ cup Tomato-Garlic Pizza Sauce (page 35)

1 cup shredded vegan mozzarella-style cheese

1 ounce fresh whole basil leaves, sliced into thin strips

1 Preheat the oven, preferably with a pizza stone inside, to 500°F for 30 minutes, while getting the pizza ready.

2 Divide your dough into 2 even pieces. Keep 1, and return 1 to the bucket, cover, and refrigerate for later use. On a lightly floured surface, stretch or roll out your dough into 1 large or 2 small rounds, as thin as you can get it. I like to make my small pizzas about 11 inches and my large between 14 and 15 inches. Don't worry if your dough tears. Simply patch it back together with your fingers. Lightly dust with additional flour if the dough is too sticky. Try not to use too much, or your crust will be very dry. Carefully transfer the rolled-out dough to a large sheet of parchment paper.

3 Spread the tomato sauce (about ¼ cup for each small pizza, and about ½ cup for a large) evenly on the pizza, leaving a ¼- to ½-inch border around the edge. Sprinkle the cheese over the sauce. If making 2 small pizzas, repeat with the remaining pizza.

4 Carefully transfer the pizza and parchment paper to the pizza stone, if using. Otherwise, place the pizza on a baking sheet, and place in the preheated oven. If making 2 small pizzas, repeat with the remaining pizza.

5 Bake for 10 to 15 minutes, until the cheese is melted and the crust looks fairly darkish brown. If it's not done, continue baking for a few more minutes.

6 Let the pizza cool for 5 minutes. Sprinkle with the basil strips before cutting into slices, and serve right away.

VARIATION: Sprinkle some fresh sliced or chopped garlic on top.

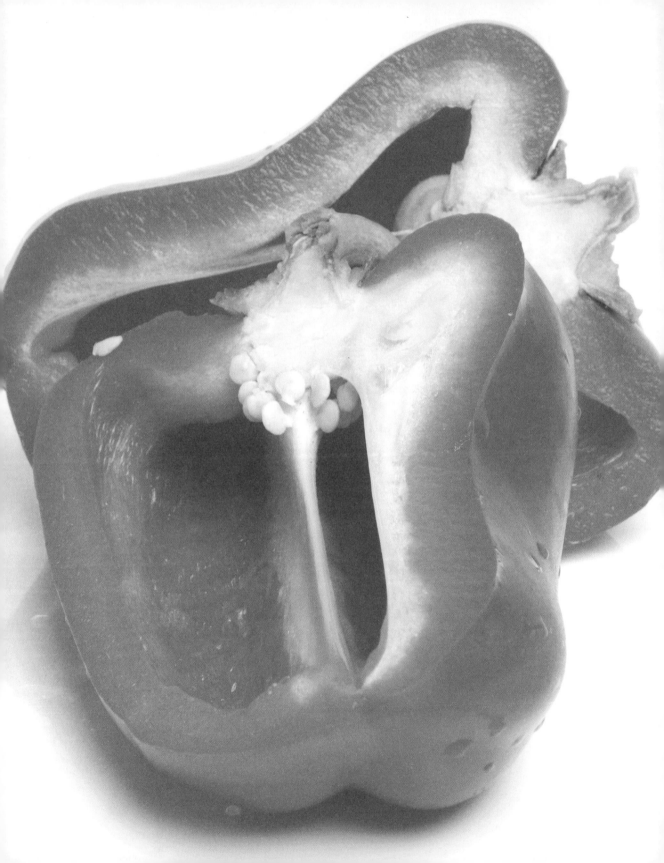

I bet you can't guess how this pizza got its name. I wanted to make a special Valentine's dinner for my husband, and I thought it would be fun to make heart-shaped pizzas, with delicious red toppings. The combination of sun-dried tomato pesto, tomatoes, and red bell peppers is so good, that it's a shame to limit it to once a year.

VALENTINE'S PIZZA

Makes **1 large** (14- to 15-inch) or **2 individual** (about 11-inch) thin-crust pizzas

1 batch pizza dough (see page 2)

½ cup Sun-Dried Tomato, Basil, and Arugula Pesto (page 32)

⅔ cup shredded vegan mozzarella-style cheese

2 red bell peppers, cored and thinly sliced

2 medium to large tomatoes, thinly sliced

1 Preheat the oven, preferably with a pizza stone inside, to 500°F for 30 minutes, while getting the pizza ready.

2 Divide your dough into 2 even pieces. Keep 1, and return 1 to the bucket, cover, and refrigerate for later use. On a lightly floured surface, stretch or roll out your dough into 1 large or 2 small heart shapes, as thin as you can get it. I like to make my small pizzas about 11 inches and my large between 14 and 15 inches, although with the heart shape the size won't be exact. Don't worry if your dough tears. Simply patch it back together with your fingers. Lightly dust with additional flour if the dough is too sticky. Try not to use too much, or your crust will be very dry. Carefully transfer the rolled-out dough to a large sheet of parchment paper.

continued on next page

3 Spread the sun-dried tomato pesto (about ¼ cup for each small pizza, and about ½ cup for a large) evenly on the pizza, leaving a ¼- to ½-inch border around the edge. Sprinkle the cheese over the sauce, and top with the bell peppers and tomatoes. If making 2 small pizzas, repeat with the remaining pizza.

4 Carefully transfer the pizza and parchment paper to the pizza stone, if using. Otherwise, place the pizza on a baking sheet, and place in the preheated oven. If making 2 small pizzas, repeat with the remaining pizza.

5 Bake for 10 to 15 minutes, until the cheese is melted and the crust looks fairly darkish brown. If it's not done, continue baking for a few more minutes.

6 Let the pizza cool for 5 minutes before cutting into slices, and serve right away.

ASPARAGUS, TOMATO, and PESTO Pizza   52

CORN, PESTO, ZUCCHINI, and TOMATO Pizza   54

MUSHROOM, BROCCOLI, and SUN-DRIED TOMATO Pizza   56

PINEAPPLE and JALAPEÑO Pizza   58

Smoky WILD MUSHROOM and POTATO Pizza   60

SWEET POTATO and KALE Pizza   62

TOMATO, CUCUMBER, and CAPER Pizza   64

FARMERS' MARKET PIZZAS

5

There's something very special about the combo of pesto and fresh asparagus. It tastes like spring to me. My daughter and I had so much fun creating this pizza one night that we decided that it needed to always be in our pizza rotation.

ASPARAGUS, TOMATO, AND PESTO PIZZA

Makes **1 large** (14- to 15-inch) pizza or **2 individual** (about 11-inch) thin-crust pizzas

1 batch pizza dough (see page 2)

½ to ⅔ cup Zesty Pesto (page 36)

⅔ cup shredded vegan mozzarella-style cheese

2 large tomatoes, thinly sliced

10 stalks asparagus, ends snapped off, cut into 3 to 4 pieces

Salt and freshly ground black pepper (optional)

1 Preheat the oven, preferably with a pizza stone inside, to 500°F for 30 minutes, while getting the pizza ready.

2 Divide your dough into 2 even pieces. Keep 1, and return 1 to the bucket, cover, and refrigerate for later use. On a lightly floured surface, stretch or roll out your dough into 1 large or 2 small rounds, as thin as you can get it. I like to make my small pizzas about 11 inches and my large between 14 and 15 inches. Don't worry if your dough tears. Simply patch it back together with your fingers. Lightly dust with additional flour if the dough is too sticky. Try not to use too much, or your crust will be very dry. Carefully transfer the rolled-out dough to a large sheet of parchment paper.

3 Spread the pesto (¼ to ⅓ cup for each small pizza, and ½ to ⅔ cup for a large) evenly on the pizza, leaving a ¼- to ½-inch border around the edge. Sprinkle the cheese over the sauce, and top with the tomatoes and asparagus. If making 2 small pizzas, repeat with the remaining pizza. If desired, sprinkle the tomatoes with salt and freshly ground black pepper.

4 Carefully transfer the pizza and parchment paper to the pizza stone, if using. Otherwise, place the pizza on a baking sheet, and place in the preheated oven. If making 2 small pizzas, repeat with the remaining pizza.

5 Bake for 10 minutes, or until the cheese is melted and the crust looks fairly darkish brown. If it's not done, continue baking for a few more minutes.

6 Let the pizza cool for 5 minutes before cutting into slices, and serve right away.

TIP: If you aren't familiar with snapping the ends off asparagus, here is how you do it. Take a stalk of raw asparagus and hold it in the middle with one hand, and with the other hand snap off the woody end piece. Alternatively, you can use a knife and cut off the bottom inch or inch and a half.

My daughter and I created this pizza one evening, after a fun adventure at our local farmers' market. Although this pizza screams with the fabulous flavors of summer, you can make it any time of year with frozen organic sweet corn.

CORN, PESTO, ZUCCHINI, AND TOMATO PIZZA

Makes **1 large** (14- to 15-inch) pizza or **2 individual** (about 11-inch) thin-crust pizzas

1 batch pizza dough (see page 2)

½ to ⅔ cup Zesty Pesto (page 36)

⅔ cup shredded vegan mozzarella-style cheese

2 small to medium zucchini, thinly sliced lengthwise and cut into 2-inch pieces

2 large tomatoes, thinly sliced

2 cups fresh sweet corn kernels, or frozen sweet organic, thawed and drained

Coarse salt and freshly ground black pepper

1 Preheat the oven, preferably with a pizza stone inside, to 500°F for 30 minutes, while getting the pizza ready.

2 Divide your dough into 2 even pieces. Keep 1, and return 1 to the bucket, cover, and refrigerate for later use. On a lightly floured surface, stretch or roll out your dough into 1 large or 2 small rounds, as thin as you can get it. I like to make my small pizzas about 11 inches and my large between 14 and 15 inches. Don't worry if your dough tears. Simply patch it back together with your fingers. Lightly dust with additional flour if the dough is too sticky. Try not to use too much, or your crust will be very dry. Carefully transfer the rolled-out dough to a large sheet of parchment paper.

3 Spread the pesto (¼ to ⅓ cup for each small pizza, and ½ to ⅔ cup for a large) evenly on the pizza, leaving a ¼- to ½-inch border around the edge. Sprinkle the cheese over the sauce, and top with the zucchini, tomatoes, and corn. If making 2 small pizzas, repeat with the remaining pizza. Sprinkle the top of the pizza with a little coarse salt and freshly ground black pepper.

4 Carefully transfer the pizza and parchment paper to the pizza stone, if using. Otherwise, place the pizza on a baking sheet, and place in the preheated oven. If making 2 small pizzas, repeat with the remaining pizza.

5 Bake for 10 to 15 minutes, or until the cheese is melted and the crust looks fairly darkish brown. If it's not done, continue baking for a few more minutes.

6 Let the pizza cool for 5 minutes before cutting into slices, and serve right away.

This is a delectable pizza, with toppings that are available all year long. That doesn't mean that it can't be enjoyed in the hot summer months, but it's always nice to have a handful of winter go-to recipes. Make sure not to bake the pizza with the sun-dried tomatoes on top, or else they will burn into little bits, as will the pine nuts.

MUSHROOM, BROCCOLI, AND SUN-DRIED TOMATO PIZZA

Makes **1 large** (14- to 15-inch) pizza or **2 individual** (about 11-inch) thin-crust pizzas

1 batch pizza dough (see page 2)

½ to ⅔ cup Tomato-Garlic Pizza Sauce (page 35)

⅔ cup shredded vegan mozzarella-style cheese

4 to 5 ounces broccoli florets, chopped into smaller pieces

4 ounces cremini mushrooms, thinly sliced

½ cup sun-dried tomato strips (soft-dried, or oil packed and drained)

⅛ cup pine nuts, toasted

1 Preheat the oven, preferably with a pizza stone inside, to 500°F for 30 minutes, while getting the pizza ready.

2 Divide your dough into 2 even pieces. Keep 1, and return 1 to the bucket, cover, and refrigerate for later use. On a lightly floured surface, stretch or roll out your dough into 1 large or 2 small rounds, as thin as you can get it. I like to make my small pizzas about 11 inches and my large between 14 and 15 inches. Don't worry if your dough tears. Simply patch it back together with your fingers. Lightly dust with additional flour if the dough is too sticky. Try not to use too much, or your crust will be very dry. Carefully transfer the rolled-out dough to a large sheet of parchment paper.

3 Spread the tomato sauce (¼ to ⅓ cup for each small pizza, and ½ to ⅔ cup for a large) evenly on the pizza, leaving a ¼- to ½-inch border around the edge. Sprinkle the cheese over the sauce, and top with the broccoli and mushrooms. If making 2 small pizzas, repeat with the remaining pizza. Carefully transfer the pizza and parchment paper to the pizza stone, if using. Otherwise, place the pizza on a baking sheet, and place in the preheated oven. If making 2 small pizzas, repeat with the remaining pizza.

4 Bake for 10 to 15 minutes, or until the cheese is melted and the crust looks fairly darkish brown. If it's not done, continue baking for a few more minutes.

5 Sprinkle the top of the pizza with the sun-dried tomatoes and pine nuts. Let the pizza cool for 5 minutes before cutting into slices, and serve right away.

TIP: To toast pine nuts, heat a small skillet over medium to medium-high heat. Add the pine nuts, and heat until they are lightly toasted, stirring or tossing them as needed. Remove from the pan and let cool.

For years I was under the impression that adding pineapple to pizza was blasphemous. Boy, was I wrong! The combination of fresh pineapple, cilantro, jalapeños, and Sweet and Smoky Soy Curls (page 25) is amazing together.

PINEAPPLE AND JALAPEÑO PIZZA

Makes **1 large** (14- to 15-inch) pizza or **2 individual** (about 11-inch) thin-crust pizzas

1 batch pizza dough (see page 2)

½ cup Tomato-Garlic Pizza Sauce (page 35)

¾ to 1 cup shredded vegan mozzarella-style cheese

About 1 cup diced fresh pineapple, or more as desired

2 jalapeños, thinly sliced

About 1 cup Sweet and Smoky Soy Curls (page 25), or 2 to 3 store-bought vegan sausages, cut into slices

Chopped fresh cilantro, for garnish

1 Preheat the oven, preferably with a pizza stone inside, to 500°F for 30 minutes, while getting the pizza ready.

2 Divide your dough into 2 even pieces. Keep 1, and return 1 to the bucket, cover, and refrigerate for later use. On a lightly floured surface, stretch or roll out your dough into 1 large or 2 small rounds, as thin as you can get it. I like to make my small pizzas about 11 inches and my large between 14 and 15 inches. Don't worry if your dough tears. Simply patch it back together with your fingers. Lightly dust with additional flour if the dough is too sticky. Try not to use too much, or your crust will be very dry. Carefully transfer the rolled-out dough to a large sheet of parchment paper.

3 Spread the tomato sauce (about ¼ cup for each small pizza, and about ½ cup for a large) evenly on the pizza, leaving a ¼- to ½-inch border around the edge. Sprinkle the cheese over the sauce, and top with the pineapple, jalapeños, and Soy Curls. If making 2 small pizzas, repeat with the remaining pizza.

4 Carefully transfer the pizza and parchment paper to the pizza stone, if using. Otherwise, place the pizza on a baking sheet, and place in the preheated oven. If making 2 small pizzas, repeat with the remaining pizza.

5 Bake for 10 to 15 minutes, until the cheese is melted and the crust looks fairly darkish brown. If it's not done, continue baking for a few more minutes.

6 Let the pizza cool for 5 minutes. Sprinkle the chopped cilantro on top, cut into slices, and serve right away.

VARIATION: Substitute any of the crumble recipes (see pages 14–21) for the Soy Curls.

TIP: The Sweet and Smoky Soy Curls can be left off, if you are so inclined.

One bite of this pizza, and I instantly fell in love. The smoky cheese sauce combined with the shiitake mushrooms and truffle oil is out-of-this-world delicious. Make sure to cut your potato slices paper-thin. If you have a mandoline for slicing, this is a perfect reason to use it.

SMOKY WILD MUSHROOM AND POTATO PIZZA

Makes **1 large** (14- to 15-inch) pizza or **2 individual** (about 11-inch) thin-crust pizzas

1 batch pizza dough (see page 2)

⅔ cup Smoky White Cheese Sauce (page 30)

⅔ cup shredded vegan mozzarella-style cheese (optional)

3 to 4 small red potatoes, cut into paper-thin slices

Salt and freshly ground black pepper

4 ounces shiitake or cremini mushrooms, thinly sliced

Finely minced fresh parsley, for garnish

Truffle oil, for garnish

1 Preheat the oven, preferably with a pizza stone inside, to 500°F for 30 minutes, while getting the pizza ready.

2 Divide your dough into 2 even pieces. Keep 1, and return 1 to the bucket, cover, and refrigerate for later use. On a lightly floured surface, stretch or roll out your dough into 1 large or 2 small rounds, as thin as you can get it. I like to make my small pizzas about 11 inches and my large between 14 and 15 inches. Don't worry if your dough tears. Simply patch it back together with your fingers. Lightly dust with additional flour if the dough is too sticky. Try not to use too much, or your crust will be very dry. Carefully transfer the rolled-out dough to a large sheet of parchment paper.

3 Spread the cheese sauce (about ⅓ cup for each small pizza, and about ⅔ cup for a large) evenly on the pizza, leaving a ¼- to ½-inch border around the edge. Sprinkle the cheese over the sauce, and top with the potatoes. Sprinkle a little salt and freshly ground black pepper over the potatoes. Scatter the mushrooms over the potatoes. If making 2 small pizzas, repeat with the remaining pizza.

4 Carefully transfer the pizza and parchment paper to the pizza stone, if using. Otherwise, place the pizza on a baking sheet, and place in the preheated oven. If making 2 small pizzas, repeat with the remaining pizza.

5 Bake for 10 to 15 minutes, or until the cheese is melted and the crust looks fairly darkish brown. If it's not done, continue baking for a few more minutes.

6 Let the pizza cool for 5 minutes. Sprinkle the top of the pizza with the minced parsley and drizzle with the truffle oil. Cut the pizza into slices and serve right away.

TIP: Brushing the potatoes with just a little olive oil will help them crisp up nicely while baking.

Here you've got a fantastically delicious farmers' market pizza. It's also healthy and full of antioxidants. A whole wheat or spelt dough (see page 8) pairs really well with the earthy flavors of the sweet potato and kale.

SWEET POTATO AND KALE PIZZA

Makes **1 large** (14- to 15-inch) pizza or **2 individual** (about 11-inch) thin-crust pizzas

1 batch pizza dough (see page 2)

½ sweet potato, peeled and very thinly sliced

1 tablespoon extra virgin olive oil, or as needed

½ cup Smoky White Cheese Sauce (page 30)

2 ounces baby kale leaves or 2 ounces chopped and destemmed large kale leaves

Salt and freshly ground black pepper

1 Preheat the oven, preferably with a pizza stone inside, to 500°F for 30 minutes, while getting the pizza ready.

2 Divide your dough into 2 even pieces. Keep 1, and return 1 to the bucket, cover, and refrigerate for later use. On a lightly floured surface, stretch or roll out your dough into 1 large or 2 small rounds, as thin as you can get it. I like to make my small pizzas about 11 inches and my large between 14 and 15 inches. Don't worry if your dough tears. Simply patch it back together with your fingers. Lightly dust with additional flour if the dough is too sticky. Try not to use too much, or your crust will be very dry. Carefully transfer the rolled-out dough to a large sheet of parchment paper.

3 In a small bowl, place the sweet potato slices. Drizzle with the olive oil and toss until the potato slices are coated.

4 Spread the cheese sauce (about ¼ cup for each small pizza, and about ½ cup for a large) evenly on the pizza, leaving a ¼- to ½-inch border around the edge. Cover the pizza with the kale and then top with a slightly overlapping layer of the sweet potatoes. Sprinkle the top with a pinch of salt and some freshly ground black pepper. If making 2 small pizzas, repeat with the remaining pizza.

5 Carefully transfer the pizza and parchment paper to the pizza stone, if using. Otherwise, place the pizza on a baking sheet, and place in the preheated oven. If making 2 small pizzas, repeat with the remaining pizza.

6 Bake for 10 to 15 minutes, or until the crust looks fairly darkish brown. If it's not done, continue baking for a few more minutes.

7 Let the pizza cool for 5 minutes before cutting into slices, and serve right away.

VARIATION: Substitute thinly sliced red potato for the sweet potato.

My daughter calls this a bagel schmear pizza, because it's all of the goodness of a fully loaded bagel, but on a pizza crust. The pizza would be a fun addition to a weekend brunch, or a perfect summer dinner with beautiful ripe heirloom tomatoes.

TOMATO, CUCUMBER, AND CAPER PIZZA

Makes **1 large** (14- to 15-inch) pizza or **2 individual** (about 11-inch) thin-crust pizzas

DILL SCHMEAR

12 ounces non-dairy soy sour cream (such as Tofutti)

2 teaspoons dried parsley flakes

1½ teaspoons granulated garlic

1½ teaspoons granulated onion

½ teaspoon fine sea salt

1 teaspoon dried dill weed

PIZZA

1 batch pizza dough (see page 2)

3 to 4 tablespoons capers

1 hothouse cucumber, thinly sliced

About 2 large tomatoes, thinly sliced

¼ red onion, thinly sliced

Salt and freshly ground black pepper

Chopped fresh dill, for garnish

1 Preheat the oven, preferably with a pizza stone inside, to 500°F for 30 minutes, while getting the pizza ready.

2 To make the dill schmear, combine the sour cream, parsley flakes, granulated garlic, granulated onion, salt, and dill in a bowl. Stir until smooth, and set aside.

3 To make the pizza, divide your dough into 2 even pieces. Keep 1, and return 1 to the bucket, cover, and refrigerate for later use. On a lightly floured surface, stretch or roll out your dough into 1 large or 2 small rounds, as thin as you can get it. I like to make my small pizzas about 11 inches and my large between 14 and 15 inches. Don't worry if your dough tears. Simply patch it back together with your fingers. Lightly dust with additional flour if the dough is too sticky. Try not to use too much, or your crust will be very dry.

4 Carefully transfer the pizza to the pizza stone, if using. Otherwise, place the pizza on a parchment-lined baking sheet, and place in the preheated oven. If making 2 small pizzas, repeat with the remaining pizza.

continued on next page

5 Bake for 10 to 15 minutes, until nicely browned. Remove from the oven and set aside to cool completely.

6 Spread the dill schmear (about ¼ cup for each small pizza, and about ½ cup for a large) evenly over the cooled crust, leaving a ¼- to ½-inch border around the edge. Sprinkle with the capers. Place a single layer of cucumber slices evenly over the dill spread. Top with the tomato slices and then the red onion slices. Sprinkle a pinch of salt and a few grinds of freshly ground black pepper over the tomato and cucumber slices. Lightly sprinkle fresh dill over the top.

7 Cut the pizza into slices and serve right away.

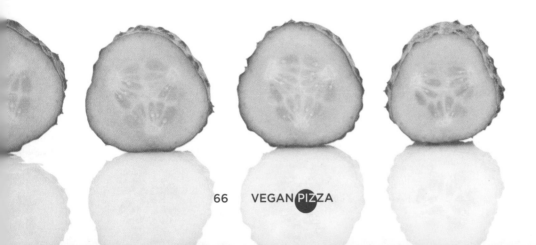

NOT YOUR USUAL SUSPECTS

If you have a mandoline hiding in the depths of your cupboard, this is a great recipe to pull it out for. A mandoline creates super-thin slices of potatoes (almost see-through) that bake up perfectly on the top of this casserole-inspired pizza. This pizza is very popular with kids too.

SCALLOPED POTATO PIZZA

Makes **1 large**
(14- to 15-inch) pizza or
2 individual (about 11-inch)
thin-crust pizzas

1 batch pizza dough (see page 2)

⅔ cup Cheddary Cashew Cheese Sauce (page 28)

1 cup shredded vegan Cheddar- or mozzarella-style cheese

6 small red potatoes, or more as needed, cut into paper-thin slices

Thinly sliced scallions, for garnish

1 Preheat the oven, preferably with a pizza stone inside, to 500°F for 30 minutes, while getting the pizza ready.

2 Divide your dough into 2 even pieces. Keep 1, and return 1 to the bucket, cover, and refrigerate for later use. On a lightly floured surface, stretch or roll out your dough into 1 large or 2 small rounds, as thin as you can get it. I like to make my small pizzas about 11 inches and my large between 14 and 15 inches. Don't worry if your dough tears. Simply patch it back together with your fingers. Lightly dust with additional flour if the dough is too sticky. Try not to use too much, or your crust will be very dry. Carefully transfer the rolled-out dough to a large sheet of parchment paper.

3 Spread the cheese sauce (about ⅓ cup for each small pizza, and about ⅔ cup for a large) evenly on the pizza, leaving a ¼- to ½-inch border around the edge. Sprinkle the cheese over the sauce, and top with an even layer of the potatoes, just slightly overlapping in a concentric circle (see tip on page 61). If making 2 small pizzas, repeat with the remaining pizza.

4 Carefully transfer the pizza and parchment paper to the pizza stone, if using. Otherwise, place the pizza on a baking sheet, and place in the preheated oven. If making 2 small pizzas, repeat with the remaining pizza.

5 Bake for 10 to 15 minutes, until the cheese is melted and the crust looks fairly darkish brown. If it's not done, continue baking for a few more minutes.

6 Let the pizza cool for 5 minutes. Sprinkle the top of the pizza with scallions, cut into slices, and serve right away.

VARIATION: You can also add chopped broccoli to this pizza or sprinkle the top with Sweet and Smoky Soy Curls (page 25).

TIP: If you have extra time, the Dill Schmear, from the Tomato, Cucumber, and Caper Pizza (page 64), is lovely with this pizza. You can either thin it a little and drizzle it on the top of the pizza, or serve it with a dollop on the side.

Broccoli and Cheddar go together like Fred and Ginger. This classic pairing of flavors has universal appeal, whether you're three or ninety-three. Sometimes you just feel like a classic, nothing too fancy, just pure comfort food at its best.

BROCCOLI AND CHEDDAR PIZZA

Makes **1 large** (14- to 15-inch) pizza or **2 individual** (about 11-inch) thin-crust pizzas

1 batch pizza dough (see page 2)

½ cup Cheddary Cashew Cheese Sauce (page 28)

1 cup shredded vegan Cheddar- or mozzarella-style cheese

4 ounces broccoli florets, chopped into small pieces

Dried red chili flakes (optional)

1 Preheat the oven, preferably with a pizza stone inside, to 500°F for 30 minutes, while getting the pizza ready.

2 Divide your dough into 2 even pieces. Keep 1, and return 1 to the bucket, cover, and refrigerate for later use. On a lightly floured surface, stretch or roll out your dough into 1 large or 2 small rounds, as thin as you can get it. I like to make my small pizzas about 11 inches and my large between 14 and 15 inches. Don't worry if your dough tears. Simply patch it back together with your fingers. Lightly dust with additional flour if the dough is too sticky. Try not to use too much, or your crust will be very dry. Carefully transfer the rolled-out dough to a large sheet of parchment paper.

3 Spread the cheese sauce (about ¼ cup for each small pizza, and about ½ cup for a large) evenly on the pizza, leaving a ¼- to ½-inch border around the edge. Sprinkle the cheese over the sauce, and top with the broccoli and chili flakes, if using. If making 2 small pizzas, repeat with the remaining pizza.

4 Carefully transfer the pizza and parchment paper to the pizza stone, if using. Otherwise, place the pizza on a baking sheet, and place in the preheated oven. If making 2 small pizzas, repeat with the remaining pizza.

5 Bake for 10 to 15 minutes, or until the cheese is melted and the crust looks fairly darkish brown. If it's not done, continue baking for a few more minutes.

6 Let the pizza cool for 5 minutes before cutting into slices, and serve right away.

This family favorite contains all of the delicious elements of a cheeseburger, layered up and served on a crispy pizza crust. Not only is this pizza kid-friendly, but it is loved by adults too, transporting them back to childhood.

CHEESEBURGER PIZZA

Makes 1 large 14-inch pizza

1 batch pizza dough (see page 2)

½ cup Tomato-Garlic Pizza Sauce (page 35)

¾ cup shredded vegan mozzarella- or Cheddar-style cheese

About 2 cups Burger Crumbles (page 14)

½ small to medium yellow onion, thinly sliced

1 (24-ounce) jar kosher dill pickle slices, drained

Yellow mustard, for garnish

Ketchup, for garnish

1 Preheat the oven, preferably with a pizza stone inside, to 500°F for 30 minutes, while getting the pizza ready.

2 Divide your dough into 2 even pieces. Keep 1, and return 1 to the bucket, cover, and refrigerate for later use. On a lightly floured surface, stretch or roll out your dough into 1 large 14-inch round. Don't worry if your dough tears. Simply patch it back together with your fingers. Lightly dust with additional flour if the dough is too sticky. Try not to use too much, or your crust will be very dry. Carefully transfer the rolled-out dough to a large sheet of parchment paper.

3 Spread the sauce evenly on the pizza, leaving a ¼- to ½-inch border around the edge. Sprinkle the cheese evenly over the sauce. Put a nice thicker layer of the Burger Crumbles evenly over the cheese. Sprinkle the onion over the cheese, and top with the pickles. I like a lot of pickles on this pizza.

4 Carefully transfer the pizza and parchment paper to the pizza stone, if using. Otherwise, place the pizza on a baking sheet, and place in the preheated oven. Bake for 10 to 15 minutes, until the cheese is melted and the crust looks fairly darkish brown. If it's not done, continue baking for a few more minutes.

5 Let the pizza cool for 5 minutes. Drizzle with yellow mustard, cut into pieces, and serve right away. If desired, drizzle the pizza with ketchup too. Alternatively, you can serve mustard and ketchup on the side.

This fantastic recipe comes to you from the awesome all-vegan barbecue cart, Homegrown Smoker, in Portland, Oregon. Jeff Ridabock created this amazing pizza, which we just couldn't get enough of.

CHILI MAC PIZZA

Makes 1 large 13- to
15-inch pizza

10 ounces cooked macaroni noodles

1½ cups Creamy Cheese Sauce (page 29) or Cheddary Cashew Cheese Sauce (page 28), or more as needed

1 (14.7- to 15-ounce) can vegetarian chili

1 batch pizza dough (see page 2)

About ¾ cup shredded vegan mozzarella-style cheese

Diced onion, for garnish

Chopped corn chips, for garnish

Diced jalapeño, for garnish

1 Preheat the oven, preferably with a pizza stone inside, to 500°F for 30 minutes, while getting the pizza ready.

2 In a small bowl, toss together the cooked pasta and enough of the cheese sauce so that it's nice and saucy. Set aside. In a small saucepan over medium heat, bring the chili to a simmer, stirring occasionally. Once it comes to a simmer, remove from the heat.

3 Divide your dough into 2 even pieces. Keep 1, and return 1 to the bucket, cover, and refrigerate for later use. On a lightly floured surface, stretch or roll out your dough into 1 large 13- to 15-inch

round. Don't worry if your dough tears. Simply patch it back together with your fingers. Lightly dust with additional flour if the dough is too sticky. Try not to use too much, or your crust will be very dry. Carefully transfer the rolled-out dough to a large sheet of parchment paper.

4 Sprinkle the cheese evenly over the crust, leaving a ½-inch border. Spread the macaroni over the cheese, leaving a ¼- to ½-inch border around the edge. If it won't all fit, that's okay. Spread or dollop the chili over the macaroni.

5 Carefully transfer the pizza and parchment paper to the pizza stone, if using. Otherwise, place the pizza on a baking sheet, and place in the preheated oven. Bake for 10 to 20 minutes, and check the pizza. You want the cheese to be melted and the crust to look nicely brown. If it's not done, continue baking for a few more minutes.

6 If desired, sprinkle the pizza with the diced onion, chopped corn chips, and diced jalapeño.

7 Let the pizza cool for 5 minutes, cut into slices, and serve right away. Serve any remaining cheese sauce on the side for drizzling, if desired.

VARIATION: **Skip the chili, corn chips, jalapeño, and onion, and make it a straight-up mac and cheese pie.**

I have to believe that if cowboys were vegan, this would be their pizza of choice. Bold, smoky, and a little spicy, there is nothing like a little barbecue sauce, jalapeño, and Cheddar to get you going.

COWBOY PIZZA

Makes **1 large** (14- to 15-inch) pizza or **2 individual** (about 11-inch) thin-crust pizzas

1 batch pizza dough (see page 2)

½ cup barbecue sauce

1 cup shredded vegan Cheddar- or mozzarella-style cheese

1½ cups Sweet and Smoky Soy Curls (page 25), or store-bought vegan crumbles, or 2 to 3 vegan sausages, cut into slices

4 ounces broccoli florets, chopped into smaller pieces

1 to 2 jalapeños, thinly sliced (optional)

About 2 tablespoons chopped fresh cilantro, for garnish

1 Preheat the oven, preferably with a pizza stone inside, to 500°F for 30 minutes, while getting the pizza ready.

2 Divide your dough into 2 even pieces. Keep 1, and return 1 to the bucket, cover, and refrigerate for later use. On a lightly floured surface, stretch or roll out your dough into 1 large or 2 small rounds, as thin as you can get it. I like to make my small pizzas about 11 inches and my large between 14 and 15 inches. Don't worry if your dough tears. Simply patch it back together with your fingers. Lightly dust with additional flour if the dough is too sticky. Try not to use too much, or your crust will be very dry.

Carefully transfer the rolled-out dough to a large sheet of parchment paper.

3 Spread the barbecue sauce (about ¼ cup for each small pizza, and about ½ cup for a large) evenly on the pizza, leaving a ¼- to ½-inch border around the edge. Sprinkle the cheese over the sauce, and top with the Soy Curls. Sprinkle the broccoli and jalapeños, if using, over the Soy Curls. If making 2 small pizzas, repeat with the remaining pizza.

4 Carefully transfer the pizza and parchment paper to the pizza stone, if using. Otherwise, place the pizza on a baking sheet, and place in the preheated oven. If making 2 small pizzas, repeat with the remaining pizza.

5 Bake for 10 to 15 minutes, until the cheese is melted and the crust looks fairly darkish brown. If it's not done, continue baking for a few more minutes.

6 Let the pizza cool for 5 minutes. Sprinkle the chopped cilantro on top, cut into slices, and serve right away.

TIP: The Sweet And Smoky Soy Curls can be left off, if desired.

Before you roll your eyes at this pizza, let me tell you that it's delicious! The rich flavor of the creamy peanut butter blended with the bold flavor of barbecue sauce is a perfect match, especially when topped with cilantro, cheese, corn, green bell pepper, and onion.

PEANUT BARBECUE
PIZZA

Makes **1 large** (14- to 15-inch) pizza or **2 individual** (about 11-inch) thin-crust pizzas

¼ cup natural peanut butter, smooth or chunky

¼ cup barbecue sauce, plus extra for garnish

1 tablespoon very hot water

1 teaspoon pure maple syrup

2 cloves garlic, minced

Dash of cayenne pepper or dried red chili flakes

1 batch pizza dough (see page 2)

¾ to 1 cup shredded vegan mozzarella-style cheese

1 large green bell pepper, cored and thinly sliced

About ⅓ yellow onion, thinly sliced

1 cup fresh sweet corn kernels, or frozen sweet organic corn kernels, thawed and drained

Chopped fresh cilantro, for garnish

1 Preheat the oven, preferably with a pizza stone inside, to 500°F for 30 minutes, while getting the pizza ready.

2 In a small or medium bowl, combine the peanut butter, barbecue sauce, hot water, maple syrup, garlic, and cayenne. Stir until the sauce is smooth and creamy. Set aside.

3 Divide your dough into 2 even pieces. Keep 1, and return 1 to the bucket, cover, and refrigerate for later use. On a lightly floured surface, stretch or roll out your dough into 1 large or 2 small rounds, as thin as you can get it. I like to make my small pizzas about 11 inches and my large between 14 and 15 inches. Don't worry if your dough tears. Simply patch it back together with your fingers. Lightly dust with additional flour if the dough is too sticky. Try not to use too much, or your crust will be very dry. Carefully transfer the rolled-out dough to a large sheet of parchment paper.

4 Spread the peanut barbecue sauce (about ¼ cup for each small pizza, and about ½ cup for a large) evenly on the pizza, leaving a ¼- to ½-inch border around the edge. Sprinkle the cheese over the sauce, and top with the green bell pepper. Scatter the onion and corn over the top. Generously sprinkle the chopped cilantro over the corn. If making 2 small pizzas, repeat with the remaining pizza.

5 Carefully transfer the pizza and parchment paper to the pizza stone, if using. Otherwise, place the pizza on a baking sheet, and place in the preheated oven. If making 2 small pizzas, repeat with the remaining pizza.

6 Bake for 10 to 15 minutes, until the cheese is melted and the crust looks fairly darkish brown. If it's not done, continue baking for a few more minutes.

7 Let the pizza cool for 5 minutes. If desired, drizzle a little barbecue sauce decoratively over the pizza, or serve it on the side. Cut into slices and serve right away.

TIP: Although I love homemade barbecue sauce, I often keep a bottle of store-bought in my refrigerator for quick dinners. The brand that I usually buy is Bull's-Eye, as it's got the right amount of tangy, savory, and sweet flavors.

There are times when you want a nice hearty pizza for dinner, especially when it's topped with broccoli, Cheddar, and some savory meaty crumbles. I like to imagine that if there was a vegan pub in town, this pizza would be their specialty.

PUB PIZZA

Makes **1 large** (14- to 15-inch) pizza or **2 individual** (about 11-inch) thin-crust pizzas

1 batch pizza dough (see page 2)

½ cup Cheddary Cashew Cheese Sauce (page 28)

¾ to 1 cup shredded vegan Cheddar- or mozzarella-style cheese

About 2 cups Burger Crumbles (page 14) or store-bought vegan crumbles

½ red onion, thinly sliced

4 ounces broccoli florets, chopped into small pieces

1 Preheat the oven, preferably with a pizza stone inside, to 500°F for 30 minutes, while getting the pizza ready.

2 Divide your dough into 2 even pieces. Keep 1, and return 1 to the bucket, cover, and refrigerate for later use. On a lightly floured surface, stretch or roll out your dough into 1 large or 2 small rounds, as thin as you can get it. I like to make my small pizzas about 11 inches and my large between 14 and 15 inches. Don't worry if your dough tears. Simply patch it back together with your fingers. Lightly dust with additional flour if the dough is too sticky. Try not to use too much, or your crust will be very dry. Carefully transfer the rolled-out dough to a large sheet of parchment paper.

3 Spread the cheese sauce (about ¼ cup for each small pizza, and about ½ cup for a large) evenly on the pizza, leaving a ¼- to ½-inch border around the edge. Sprinkle the cheese over the sauce, and top with a generous layer of the Burger Crumbles. Scatter the onion and broccoli over the crumbles. If making 2 small pizzas, repeat with the remaining pizza.

4 Carefully transfer the pizza and parchment paper to the pizza stone, if using. Otherwise, place the pizza on a baking sheet, and place in the preheated oven. If making 2 small pizzas, repeat with the remaining pizza.

5 Bake for 10 to 15 minutes, until the cheese is melted and the crust looks fairly darkish brown. If it's not done, continue baking for a few more minutes.

6 Let the pizza cool for 5 minutes before cutting into slices, and serve right away.

This recipe comes from my friend Kittee Berns, who makes the best muffuletta pizza, dripping with chopped olives, herbs, and pickled vegetables. The recipe makes more olive salad than you will actually need for the pizza, but fear not, as you can serve the extra salad on the side or pile your pizza with even more than the recipe calls for. This is a fabulous nod to New Orleans, Kittee-style!

MUFFULETTA PIZZA

Makes **1 large** (14- to 15-inch) pizza or **2 individual** (about 11-inch) thin-crust pizzas

OLIVE SALAD

⅓ cup extra virgin olive oil

2 tablespoons coarsely chopped fresh parsley

1 (16-ounce) jar giardiniera, rinsed and drained

½ cup garlic-stuffed green olives

½ cup pimiento-stuffed green olives

½ cup pitted Kalamata olives

2 tablespoons capers

¼ teaspoon dried oregano

¼ teaspoon dried marjoram

Freshly ground black pepper

PIZZA

1 batch pizza dough (see page 2)

½ cup Tomato-Garlic Pizza Sauce (page 35)

⅔ cup Garlic Soy Curls (page 22; optional)

Extra virgin olive oil, for garnish

Dried red chili flakes (optional)

1 Preheat the oven, preferably with a pizza stone inside, to 500°F for 30 minutes, while getting the pizza ready.

2 To make the olive salad, combine the olive oil and parsley in the bowl of a food processor and pulse until the parsley is minced. Add the giardiniera, olives, capers, oregano, and marjoram, and pulse 2 to 3 times until coarsely chopped, but still very chunky. Add black pepper to taste, and set aside.

3 To make the pizza, divide your dough into 2 even pieces. Keep 1, and return 1 to the bucket, cover, and refrigerate for later use. On a lightly floured surface, stretch or roll out your dough into 1 large or 2 small rounds, as thin as you can get it. I like to make my small pizzas about 11 inches and my large between 14 and 15 inches. Don't worry if your dough tears. Simply patch it back together with your fingers. Lightly dust with additional flour if the dough is too sticky. Try not to use too much, or your crust will be very dry. Carefully transfer the rolled-out dough to a large sheet of parchment paper.

continued on next page

4 Spread the tomato sauce (about ¼ cup for each small pizza, and about ½ cup for a large) evenly on the pizza, leaving a ¼- to ½-inch border around the edge. Sprinkle the olive salad (about ¾ cup for each small pizza, and about 1½ cups for a large) over the tomato sauce. Sprinkle the Garlic Soy Curls over the olive salad, if using. If making 2 small pizzas, repeat with the remaining pizza.

5 Carefully transfer the pizza and parchment paper to the pizza stone, if using. Otherwise, place the pizza on a baking sheet, and place in the preheated oven. If making 2 small pizzas, repeat with the remaining pizza.

6 Bake for 10 to 15 minutes, until the crust looks fairly darkish brown. If it's not done, continue baking for a few more minutes.

7 Drizzle the pizza with a little olive oil, cut into slices, and serve right away. Sprinkle with chili flakes, if desired. Serve additional olive salad on the side, if desired.

GLOBAL FLAVORS

7

Sometimes there is nothing like a little barbecue sauce to get the party started. Here you've got all of the savory goodness of barbecue sauce, with a crispy pizza crust, a little cheese, some tender onion, and smoky Soy Curls. Delicious!

ALL-AMERICAN
BARBECUE PIZZA

Makes **1 large** (14- to 15-inch) pizza or **2 individual** (about 11-inch) thin-crust pizzas

1 batch pizza dough (see page 2)

½ cup barbecue sauce

¾ to 1 cup shredded vegan mozzarella-style cheese

½ red onion, thinly sliced

1 cup Sweet and Smoky Soy Curls (page 25) or Garlic Soy Curls (page 22)

Chopped fresh cilantro, for garnish

1 Preheat the oven, preferably with a pizza stone inside, to 500°F for 30 minutes, while getting the pizza ready.

2 Divide your dough into 2 even pieces. Keep 1, and return 1 to the bucket, cover, and refrigerate for later use. On a lightly floured surface, stretch or roll out your dough into 1 large or 2 small rounds, as thin as you can get it. I like to make my small pizzas about 11 inches and my large between 14 and 15 inches. Don't worry if your dough tears. Simply patch it back together with your fingers. Lightly dust with additional flour if the dough is too sticky. Try not to use too much, or your crust will be very dry. Carefully transfer the rolled-out dough to a large sheet of parchment paper.

3 Spread the barbecue sauce (about ¼ cup for each small pizza, and about ½ cup for a large) evenly on the pizza, leaving a ¼- to ½-inch border around the edge. Sprinkle the cheese over the sauce, and top with the red onion and Soy Curls. If making 2 small pizzas, repeat with the remaining pizza.

4 Carefully transfer the pizza and parchment paper to the pizza stone, if using. Otherwise, place the pizza on a baking sheet, and place in the preheated oven. If making 2 small pizzas, repeat with the remaining pizza.

5 Bake for 10 to 15 minutes, until the cheese is melted and the crust looks fairly darkish brown. If it's not done, continue baking for a few more minutes.

6 Sprinkle the chopped cilantro over the pizza. Let the pizza cool for 5 minutes before cutting into slices, and serve right away.

VARIATION: Substitute Burger Crumbles (page 14) or Sausage Crumbles (page 18) for the Soy Curls.

Bibimbap is a fantastic and flavorful Korean rice dish, served topped with a variety of savory vegetables and a sweet and spicy chili paste known as gochujang sauce. This pizza has all of those elements and more, from the sweet and spicy sauce to the veggies on top.

BIBIMBAP PIZZA

Makes **1 large** (14- to 15-inch) pizza or **2 individual** (about 11-inch) thin-crust pizzas

½ cup gochujang (Korean hot red pepper paste)

2 teaspoons toasted sesame seeds

¼ cup agave nectar

4 to 5 teaspoons toasted sesame oil

2 cloves garlic, minced

1 to 2 tablespoons hot water

1 batch pizza dough (see page 2)

1 to 2 ounces baby spinach

½ to 1 cup shredded vegan mozzarella-style cheese

1 cup thinly sliced mushrooms, preferably shiitake or cremini

4 scallions, thinly sliced

2 cups bean sprouts

Toasted sesame seeds, for garnish

1 Preheat the oven, preferably with a pizza stone inside, to 500°F for 30 minutes, while getting the pizza ready.

2 In a small bowl, mix together the red pepper paste, sesame seeds, agave, 2 teaspoons of the oil, and the garlic. Add the water and stir until smooth. Set aside.

3 Divide your dough into 2 even pieces. Keep 1, and return 1 to the bucket, cover, and refrigerate for later use. On a lightly floured surface, stretch or roll out your dough into 1 large or 2 small rounds, as thin as you can get it. I like to make my small pizzas about 11 inches and my large between 14 and 15 inches. Don't worry if your dough tears. Simply patch it back together with your fingers. Lightly dust with additional flour if the dough is too sticky. Try not to use too much, or your crust will be very dry. Carefully transfer the rolled-out dough to a large sheet of parchment paper.

4 Spread the prepared sauce (about ¼ cup for each small pizza, and about ½ cup for a large) evenly on the pizza, leaving a ¼- to ½-inch border around the edge. Sprinkle the spinach leaves over the sauce. Sprinkle the cheese over the spinach, and top with the mushrooms. If making 2 small pizzas, repeat with the remaining pizza.

5 Carefully transfer the pizza and parchment paper to the pizza stone, if using. Otherwise, place the pizza on a baking sheet, and place in the preheated oven. If making 2 small pizzas, repeat with the remaining pizza.

continued on next page

6 Bake for 10 to 15 minutes, until the cheese is melted and the crust looks fairly dark brown. If it's not done, continue baking for a few more minutes.

7 While the pizza is baking, prepare the bean sprout topping: Heat a skillet over medium-high heat. Add the remaining 2 to 3 teaspoons toasted sesame oil, swirl the oil in the pan, and add the scallions. Sauté the scallions for about 30 seconds and then add the bean sprouts. Cook just until the bean sprouts wilt, and remove the pan from the heat.

8 Top the pizza with the bean sprouts and scallions, and garnish with a sprinkle of toasted sesame seeds. If making 2 small pizzas, repeat with the remaining pizza.

9 Let the pizza cool for 5 minutes before cutting into slices, and serve right away. Serve any extra sauce on the side.

SIDEBAR

Gochujang is a Korean hot red pepper paste. It is not the same as sriracha sauce, and is actually a fermented chili paste, made from glutinous rice powder mixed with powdered fermented soybeans and red peppers. The flavor is very deep and complex, and I highly recommend searching this paste out. The flavors will amaze you. You can find it at Asian markets and grocery stores, and online.

The delicate crispy edges of the crust, and the buttery texture of the eggplant, layered with tomato sauce and a light sprinkling of melted cheese, will knock your socks off!

EGGPLANT PARMESAN
PIZZA

Makes **1 large**
(12 to 13-inch) pizza
or **2 individual**
(about 9-inch) pizzas

Kosher salt

½ large eggplant, cut into ¼- to ½-inch slices

½ cup non-dairy milk

¼ cup cornstarch

1½ cups panko breadcrumbs

2 tablespoons nutritional yeast flakes

Salt and freshly ground black pepper

Olive oil, as needed

1 batch pizza dough (see page 2)

½ cup Tomato-Garlic Pizza Sauce (page 35)

¾ to 1 cup shredded vegan mozzarella-style cheese

Slivered fresh basil, for garnish

1 Sprinkle salt on both sides of each eggplant slice and set aside on a plate for 15 to 20 minutes. This will help remove any bitterness from the eggplant. You will notice that the eggplant is expressing little beads of water. That's what you want. Rinse the salt off the eggplant and pat the slices dry with a towel.

continued on next page

2 Preheat the oven, preferably with a pizza stone inside, to 500°F for 30 minutes, while getting the pizza ready.

3 In a shallow bowl, whisk together the milk and cornstarch. In a separate shallow bowl or on a plate, combine the panko crumbs, nutritional yeast, and a pinch of salt and a few grinds of black pepper.

4 Preheat a large cast-iron or nonstick skillet over medium to medium-high heat. Add 2 tablespoons olive oil, and swirl around the pan. Coat the eggplant slices with the milk mixture, then thoroughly coat with the panko crumbs, making sure to evenly coat both sides. Place the eggplant slices in the skillet, adding additional olive oil as needed. Once the eggplant is nicely browned, about 5 minutes, carefully flip the slices over, and continue cooking until the second side is nicely browned. Remove the cooked eggplant slices to a clean plate or cutting board, and set aside.

5 Divide your dough into 2 even pieces. Keep 1, and return 1 to the bucket, cover, and refrigerate for later use. On a lightly floured surface, stretch or roll out your dough into 1 large or 2 small rounds. For this particular pizza, roll the dough to about 9 inches for the smaller pizzas and about 12 to 13 inches for the large. Don't worry if your dough tears. Simply patch it back together with your fingers. Lightly dust with additional flour if the dough is too sticky. Try not to use too much, or your crust will be very dry. Carefully transfer the rolled-out dough to a large sheet of parchment paper.

6 Spread the sauce evenly on the pizza, leaving a ¼-inch border around the edge. Sprinkle the cheese over the sauce, and top with an even layer of the browned eggplant slices. You may need to cut some of the eggplant slices. If making 2 small pieces, repeat with the remaining pizza.

7 Carefully transfer the pizza and parchment paper to the preheated pizza stone, if using. Otherwise, place the pizza on a baking sheet, and place in the preheated oven. If making 2 small pizzas, repeat with the remaining pizza.

8 Bake for 10 to 15 minutes, until the cheese is melted and the crust looks fairly dark brown. If it's not done, continue baking for a few more minutes.

9 Garnish the pizza with slivered basil. Let the pizza cool for 5 minutes before cutting into slices, and serve right away.

TIP: Although most of the pizzas in this book call for a very thin crust, I prefer this crust to be slightly thicker. So when you roll it out, don't roll it quite as thin as the others.

This pizza is always wildly popular when we entertain. The combination of pesto, peppers, olives, and artichokes makes this one stupendous pizza. My son is super picky about what goes on his slice. Most often it's nothing more than plain cheese, and maybe a stray slice of onion or tomato. That is until he tried this pizza. He finished off half the pie himself!

MEDITERRANEAN
PESTO PIZZA

Makes **1 large** (14- to 15-inch) pizza or **2 individual** (about 11-inch) thin-crust pizzas

1 batch pizza dough (see page 2)

½ cup Zesty Pesto (page 36)

¾ to 1 cup shredded vegan mozzarella-style cheese

½ green bell pepper, thinly sliced

½ red bell pepper, thinly sliced

½ small yellow onion, thinly sliced

½ cup pitted Kalamata olives, sliced in half lengthwise

½ cup canned artichoke hearts, sliced in half

1 Preheat the oven, preferably with a pizza stone inside, to 500°F for 30 minutes, while getting the pizza ready.

2 Divide your dough into 2 even pieces. Keep 1, and return 1 to the bucket, cover, and refrigerate for later use. On a lightly floured surface, stretch or roll out your dough into 1 large or 2 small rounds, as thin as you can get it. I like to make my small pizzas about 11 inches and my large between 14 and 15 inches. Don't worry if your dough tears. Simply patch it back together with your fingers. Lightly dust with additional flour if the dough is too sticky. Try not to use too much, or your crust will be very dry. Carefully transfer the rolled-out dough to a large sheet of parchment paper.

3 Spread the pesto evenly on the pizza, leaving a ¼- to ½-inch border around the edge. Sprinkle the cheese over the pesto, and top with the green and red peppers, onion, olives, and artichoke hearts. If making 2 small pizzas, repeat with the remaining pizza.

4 Carefully transfer the pizza and parchment paper to the pizza stone, if using. Otherwise, place the pizza on a baking sheet, and place in the preheated oven. If making 2 small pizzas, repeat with the remaining pizza.

5 Bake for 10 to 15 minutes, until the cheese is melted and the crust looks fairly darkish brown. If it's not done, continue baking for a few more minutes.

6 Let the pizza cool for 5 minutes before cutting into slices, and serve right away.

Although tacos might traditionally be served in corn tortillas, this variation is so good, you will think this is the way that tacos are meant to be served. This is a dynamite combo, loaded with all of the essential flavors and textures. Try serving this pizza with a pitcher of chilled beer or icy margaritas.

TACO PIZZA

Makes **1 large** (14- to 15-inch) pizza or **2 individual** (about 11-inch) thin-crust pizzas

1 batch pizza dough (see page 2)

½ cup Cheddary Cashew Cheese Sauce (page 28)

⅔ cup shredded vegan mozzarella- or Cheddar-style cheese (optional)

About 2 cups Taco Crumbles (page 20) or store-bought meatless crumbles

⅓ yellow onion, thinly sliced

2 jalapeños, thinly sliced (optional)

Diced tomatoes, for garnish

Tortilla chips, for garnish

1 Preheat the oven, preferably with a pizza stone inside, to 500°F for 30 minutes, while getting the pizza ready.

2 Divide your dough into 2 even pieces. Keep 1, and return 1 to the bucket, cover, and refrigerate for later use. On a lightly floured surface, stretch or roll out your dough into 1 large or 2 small rounds, as thin as you can get it. I like to make my small pizzas about 11 inches and my large between 14 and 15 inches. Don't worry if your dough tears. Simply patch it back together with your fingers. Lightly dust with additional flour if the dough is too sticky. Try not to use too much, or your crust will be very dry.

Carefully transfer the rolled-out dough to a large sheet of parchment paper.

3 Spread the cheese sauce (about ¼ cup for each small pizza, and about ½ cup for a large) evenly on the pizza, leaving a ¼- to ½-inch border around the edge. Sprinkle the cheese, if using, evenly over the sauce. Put a nice thick layer of the Taco Crumbles evenly over the cheese. Sprinkle the onion over the cheese, and top with the jalapeños, if using. If making 2 small pizzas, repeat with the remaining pizza.

4 Carefully transfer the pizza and parchment paper to the pizza stone, if using. Otherwise, place the pizza on a baking sheet, and place in the preheated oven. If making 2 small pizzas, repeat with the remaining pizza.

5 Bake for 10 to 15 minutes, until the cheese is melted and the crust looks fairly darkish brown. If it's not done, continue baking for a few more minutes.

6 Let the pizza cool for 5 minutes. Garnish the baked pizza with diced tomatoes and tortilla chips. Cut into slices and serve right away.

TIP: Try drizzling the pizza with taco or hot sauce to really kick the flavor up a notch. Another great garnish is diced or sliced avocado.

I have been making and serving this pizza for years. The flavors are fantastic and vibrant, and it goes together really quickly. I bet you can't eat just one slice of this pizza.

THAI PEANUT PIZZA

Makes **1 large** (14- to 15-inch) pizza or **2 individual** (about 11-inch) thin-crust pizzas

⅔ cup peanut butter

⅓ cup hoisin sauce

¼ cup hot water

2 cloves garlic, minced

1 tablespoon hot sauce (such as sriracha-style)

1 tablespoon agave nectar

1 batch pizza dough (see page 2)

¾ to 1 cup shredded vegan mozzarella-style cheese

4 ounces broccoli florets, chopped into smaller pieces

1 small bunch scallions, thinly sliced, for garnish

Chopped fresh cilantro, or fresh basil leaves (or Thai basil), thinly sliced into strips, for garnish

1 Preheat the oven, preferably with a pizza stone inside, to 500°F for 30 minutes, while getting the pizza ready.

2 In a small or medium bowl, combine the peanut butter, hoisin sauce, hot water, garlic, hot sauce, and agave. Stir until the sauce is smooth and creamy. Set aside.

continued on next page

3 Divide your dough into 2 even pieces. Keep 1, and return 1 to the bucket, cover, and refrigerate for later use. On a lightly floured surface, stretch or roll out your dough into 1 large or 2 small rounds, as thin as you can get it. I like to make my small pizzas about 11 inches and my large between 14 and 15 inches. Don't worry if your dough tears. Simply patch it back together with your fingers. Lightly dust with additional flour if the dough is too sticky. Try not to use too much, or your crust will be very dry. Carefully transfer the rolled-out dough to a large sheet of parchment paper.

4 Spread the peanut sauce (about ¼ cup for each small pizza, and about ½ cup for a large) evenly on the pizza, leaving a ¼- to ½-inch border around the edge. Sprinkle the cheese over the sauce, and top with the broccoli. If making 2 small pizzas, repeat with the remaining pizza.

5 Carefully transfer the pizza and parchment paper to the pizza stone, if using. Otherwise, place the pizza on a baking sheet, and place in the preheated oven. If making 2 small pizzas, repeat with the remaining pizza.

6 Bake for 10 to 15 minutes, until the cheese is melted and the crust looks fairly darkish brown. If it's not done, continue baking for a few more minutes.

7 Let the pizza cool for 5 minutes. Sprinkle the scallions and cilantro or basil over the pizza. Cut into slices and serve right away.

SWEET PIZZA PIES

8

If you are a fan of Babka, a traditional Jewish sweet bread with a chocolate-cinnamon-swirl filling and a streusel topping, then you will love this dessert pizza! Once you make the filling and streusel, this pizza goes together really fast.

BABKA PIZZA

Makes **2 small** (8- to 9-inch) pizzas

FILLING

1 cup dairy-free semisweet chocolate chips

⅓ cup packed light brown sugar

2 tablespoons cocoa powder, preferably Dutch-processed

1 teaspoon ground cinnamon

2 tablespoons vegan, non-hydrogenated margarine (such as Earth Balance), softened

STREUSEL

⅔ cup confectioners' sugar

⅔ cup unbleached all-purpose flour (or gluten-free all-purpose flour)

4 tablespoons (¼ cup) vegan, non-hydrogenated margarine (such as Earth Balance), softened

½ teaspoon pure almond extract

PIZZA

1 batch pizza dough (or more as need to make a thicker crust; see page 2)

Confectioners' sugar, for garnish

1 Preheat the oven, preferably with a pizza stone inside, to 450°F for 30 minutes, while getting the pizza ready.

2 To make the filling, combine the chocolate chips, brown sugar, cocoa powder, cinnamon, and softened margarine in the bowl of a food processor. Pulse the mixture until it is mixed and the texture is chunky. Don't overprocess it.

3 To make the streusel, mix together the confectioners' sugar and flour in a small bowl. Add the softened margarine and almond extract. Using your fingertips, mix the margarine into the flour mixture, squeezing until a nice crumbly mixture forms.

4 To make the pizza, divide your dough into 2 even pieces. Keep 1, and return 1 to the bucket, cover, and refrigerate for later use. On a lightly floured surface, stretch or roll out your dough into two 8- to 9-inch rounds. Don't worry if your dough tears. Simply patch it back together with your fingers. Lightly dust with additional flour if the dough is too sticky. Try not to use too much, or your crust will be very dry. Carefully transfer the rolled-out dough to a large sheet of parchment paper.

5 Spread the filling evenly on the pizza, leaving a ½-inch border around the edge. Sprinkle the streusel evenly over the filling. Repeat with the remaining pizza.

continued on next page

6 Carefully transfer the pizza and parchment paper to the pizza stone, if using. Otherwise, place the pizza on a baking sheet, and place in the preheated oven. Repeat with the remaining pizza.

7 Bake for 10 to 15 minutes, until the crust is golden brown and the streusel and chocolate look somewhat melty. If it's not done, continue baking for a few more minutes.

8 Let the pizza cool for 10 minutes before slicing . This is a rich pizza, so you may want to cut smaller slices. Dust with confectioners' sugar and serve right away.

I am a pie fanatic, and the combination of the berry filling and the crisp pizza crust is just too good for words. It makes a fun ending to an all-pizza dinner and will surprise your guests with both its deliciousness and its creativity.

BERRY PIE PIZZA

Makes **2 small** (8- to 9-inch) pizzas

BERRY TOPPING

4 cups fresh or frozen boysenberries, Marionberries, raspberries, or blueberries

⅔ cup granulated sugar

½ cup cool water

¼ cup cornstarch

PIZZA

1 batch pizza dough (see page 2)

Confectioners' sugar, for garnish

1 Preheat the oven, preferably with a pizza stone inside, to 500°F for 30 minutes, while getting the pizza ready.

2 To make the topping, combine the berries, granulated sugar, and ¼ cup of the water in a large saucepan. Bring the mixture to a simmer over medium heat. Try not to stir, so as not to mash the berries. In a small bowl, whisk together the cornstarch and the remaining ¼ cup water until smooth. Stir the cornstarch mixture into the hot berries and simmer until thick and the mixture is clear, carefully stirring. Remove the saucepan from the heat.

continued on next page

3 To make the pizza, divide your dough into 2 even pieces. Keep 1, and return 1 to the bucket, cover, and refrigerate for later use. On a lightly floured surface, stretch or roll out your dough into two 8- to 9-inch rounds. The dough for this recipe is rolled a little thicker, to hold up to the berry filling. Don't worry if your dough tears. Simply patch it back together with your fingers. Lightly dust with additional flour if the dough is too sticky. Try not to use too much, or your crust will be very dry. Carefully transfer the rolled-out dough to a large sheet of parchment paper.

4 Carefully transfer the pizza and parchment paper to the pizza stone, if using. Otherwise, place the pizza on a baking sheet, and place in the preheated oven. Repeat with the remaining pizza.

5 Bake for 10 to 15 minutes, until the crust is nicely golden brown. If it's not done, continue baking for a few more minutes.

6 Spread the thickened berry mixture generously over the cooled crust. Dust with confectioners' sugar and serve right away.

Dessert pizzas are out of this world, and a super-delicious and fun dessert to serve for company. To make this dessert even easier, pre-bake the crusts earlier in the day and top them right before serving.

COCONUT-CARAMEL
PIZZA

Makes **2 small** (8- to 9-inch) pizzas

1 batch pizza dough (see page 2)

CARAMEL

¾ **cup lightly packed brown sugar**

1 tablespoon cornstarch

⅓ **cup light corn syrup**

¼ **teaspoon fine sea salt**

⅓ **cup canned coconut milk**

Sliced bananas, semisweet chocolate chips, toasted coconut, or fresh raspberries, for garnish

1 Preheat the oven, preferably with a pizza stone inside, to 450°F for 30 minutes, while getting the pizza ready.

2 Divide your dough into 2 even pieces. Keep 1, and return 1 to the bucket, cover, and refrigerate for later use. On a lightly floured surface, stretch or roll out your dough into two 8- to 9-inch rounds. The dough for this recipe is rolled a little thicker, to hold up to the filling. Don't worry if your dough tears. Simply patch it back together with your fingers. Lightly dust with additional flour if the dough is too sticky.

continued on next page

Try not to use too much, or your crust will be very dry. Carefully transfer the rolled-out dough to a large sheet of parchment paper.

3 Carefully transfer the pizza and parchment paper to the pizza stone, if using. Otherwise, place the pizza on a baking sheet, and place in the preheated oven. Repeat with remaining pizza.

4 Bake for 10 to 15 minutes, until the crust is nicely golden brown. If it's not done, continue baking for a few more minutes.

5 To make the caramel, whisk together the brown sugar and cornstarch until well mixed. Add the corn syrup, salt, and coconut milk, whisking until smooth.

6 Over medium heat, bring the sugar mixture to a simmer, whisking continuously, and simmer for 8 minutes. Remove from the heat. The caramel will thicken up as it sits and cools. Stir or whisk occasionally to keep it smooth.

7 Once the caramel is thickened, spread the caramel generously over the cooled crust. If desired, top the pizza with banana slices, chocolate chips, toasted coconut, fresh raspberries, or other desired toppings.

8 Cut the pizza into slices and serve right away.

Here I have created a chocolate-hazelnut butter, with two kinds of chocolate and roasted hazelnuts, spread on top of a crispy baked shell. I call it a breakfast of champions, but you may call it dessert. If you're in a hurry, you can cheat and use a store-bought chocolate-hazelnut butter.

CHOCOLATE-HAZELNUT
PIZZA

Makes **2 small** (8- to 9-inch) pizzas

1 batch pizza dough (see page 2)

¼ cup dairy-free semisweet chocolate chips

¼ cup plain unsweetened soy milk, or as needed

1 cup chopped roasted hazelnuts (skinned and toasted)

½ cup confectioners' sugar

2 tablespoons cocoa powder, preferably Dutch-processed

Sliced bananas, for garnish

1 Preheat the oven, preferably with a pizza stone inside, to 500°F for 30 minutes, while getting the pizza ready.

2 Divide your dough into 2 even pieces. Keep 1, and return 1 to the bucket, cover, and refrigerate for later use. On a lightly floured surface, stretch or roll out your dough into two 8- to 9-inch rounds. The dough for this recipe is rolled a little thicker, to hold up to the topping. Don't worry if your dough tears. Simply patch it back together with your fingers. Lightly dust with additional flour if the dough is too sticky. Try not to use too much, or your crust will be very dry. Carefully transfer the rolled-out dough to a large sheet of parchment paper.

continued on next page

3 Carefully transfer the pizza and parchment paper to the pizza stone, if using. Otherwise, place the pizza on a baking sheet, and place in the preheated oven. Repeat with the remaining pizza.

4 Bake for 10 to 15 minutes, until the crust is nicely golden brown. If it's not done, continue baking for a few more minutes.

5 In a small microwave-safe bowl, combine the chocolate chips and 2 tablespoons of the soy milk. Heat for 20 to 30 seconds. The chocolate chips should be warm and starting to melt. Give them a couple of stirs. If they continue melting the rest of the way, they're good. If they are only partially melted, return to the microwave and heat for another 20 seconds. Give them another couple of stirs until they are completely melted.

SIDEBAR

You can often buy already roasted hazelnuts (and even, sometimes, chopped too). I find mine at our local farmers' market or online (see Resources, page 114).

6 In the bowl of a food processor, combine the hazelnuts, confectioners' sugar, and cocoa powder. Process the nut mixture until it's finely ground, stopping and scraping down the sides as needed. This will probably take a couple of minutes, depending on your particular food processor. You want to process the mixture until it completely breaks down into nut butter. The nuts will go from being powdery to being an oily thick mixture. Once you have nut butter, add the melted chocolate mixture and pulse again, until the mixture is smooth. Add the remaining 2 tablespoons soy milk, and process until smooth. If the mixture is too thick, add a little more soy milk to thin the nut butter so that it's a spreadable consistency.

7 Spread the chocolate-hazelnut butter generously over the cooled crust. Top with sliced bananas and serve.

TIP: To toast hazelnuts, preheat the oven to 350°F. Place the hazelnuts in a single layer on a baking sheet, lined with parchment paper or a Silpat. Bake for 10 minutes, or until the skins are darkened and split and the nuts give off a toasty aroma. Check the nuts every few minutes while toasting, and shake or stir the nuts so they toast evenly. Remove the nuts and let cool slightly. Wrap the nuts in a clean kitchen towel. Rub the nuts until most of the skins come off. Some may be stubborn and not come off, but don't worry.

Pizza for dessert? Yes, please! If you can imagine a dreamy dessert being a love child between a cookie bar and pizza, this would be it. The pizza dough is spread with raspberry jam, topped with a buttery streusel, and baked until puffed and golden. It makes a lovely dessert, indeed!

RASPBERRY CRUMBLE
PIZZA

Makes **2 small** (8- to 9-inch) pizzas

CRUMBLE

¾ cup unbleached all-purpose flour (or gluten-free all-purpose flour)

½ cup old-fashioned oats

½ cup packed light brown sugar

1 teaspoon ground cinnamon

4 tablespoons (¼ cup) vegan, non-hydrogenated margarine (like Earth Balance), softened

PIZZA

1 batch pizza dough (see page 2)

About ½ cup raspberry jam

Confectioners' sugar, for garnish

1 To make the crumble, mix together the flour, oats, brown sugar, and cinnamon in a small bowl. Add the softened margarine, and using your fingertips, mix the margarine into the flour mixture, squeezing until a nice crumbly mixture forms.

2 Preheat the oven, preferably with a pizza stone inside, to 500°F for 30 minutes, while getting the pizza ready.

3 To make the pizza, divide your dough into 2 even pieces. Keep 1, and return 1 to the bucket, cover, and refrigerate for later use. On a lightly floured surface, stretch or roll out your dough into two 8- to 9-inch rounds. The dough for this recipe is rolled a little thicker, to hold up to the berry filling. Don't worry if your dough tears. Simply patch it back together with your fingers. Lightly dust with additional flour if the dough is too sticky. Try not to use too much, or your crust will be very dry. Carefully transfer the rolled-out dough to a large sheet of parchment paper.

4 Spread the jam evenly on the pizza, leaving a ¼-inch border around the edge. Sprinkle the crumble evenly over the filling. Repeat with the remaining pizza.

5 Carefully transfer the pizza and parchment paper to the pizza stone, if using. Otherwise, place the pizza on a baking sheet, and place in the preheated oven. Repeat with the remaining pizza.

6 Bake for 10 to 15 minutes, until the crumble topping and the crust are nicely browned. If it's not done, continue baking for a few more minutes.

7 Let the pizza cool for about 5 minutes before cutting into slices. This is a rich pizza, so you may want to cut smaller slices. Dust with the confectioners' sugar and serve.

TIP: This pizza is best eaten the day that it is made.

RE-SOURCES

EQUIPMENT

BLENDTEC
www.blendtec.com
1-801-222-0888
Manufacturer of high-quality, high-powered blenders.

CUISINART
www.cuisinart.com
1-800-211-9604
Manufacturer of food processors, stand mixers, blenders, countertop pizza ovens, and more.

KITCHENAID
www.kitchenaid.com
1-800-541-6390
Manufacturer of both small and large kitchen appliances, including stand mixers, food processors, and hand mixers.

LODGE
www.lodgemfg.com
1-423-837-7181
Manufacturer of excellent-quality American-made cast-iron skillets and Dutch ovens. Their Lodge Pro Logic cast-iron 14-inch pizza pan is fabulous and makes a fantastic crisp-crust pizza.

SILPAT
www.silpat.com
1-609-395-0219
Manufactured by Sasa DeMarle, Silpat, Silpain, and Roul'Pat are silicone baking mats. They are perfect for pizza making.

VITAMIX
www.vitamix.com
1-800-848-2649
Manufacturer of high-quality, high-powered blenders.

SPECIALTY FLOURS AND INGREDIENTS

AUTHENTIC FOODS

authenticfoods.com

1-800-806-4737

Fantastic gluten-free flours, including incredible superfine brown rice flour, tapioca starch, sweet rice flour, and many others.

BOB'S RED MILL NATURAL FOODS

www.bobsredmill.com

1-800-349-2173

An excellent source for freshly milled, non-GMO whole grain organic flours, gluten-free flours, starches, and TVP and TSP. I especially love their fine-grind cornmeal and sweet rice flour.

FREDDY GUY'S HAZELNUTS

www.freddyguys.com

1-503-606-0458

A hazelnut farm in Portland, Oregon, that grows and roasts their own hazelnuts. They have the freshest, most delicious hazelnuts I've ever tasted.

MADHAVA NATURAL SWEETENERS

www.madhavasweeteners.com

1-800-530-2900

They have a great line of agave nectars.

NIELSEN-MASSEY VANILLAS

www.nielsenmassey.com

1-847-578-1550

Processor of high-quality pure vanilla extracts, beans, and powders, as well as a variety of other pure extracts.

SAF/RED STAR YEAST

www.redstaryeast.com

1-800-445-4746

This is a great website loaded with information about baking with yeast, the science of yeast, tips and troubleshooting, and nutritional yeast.

SOY CURLS

www.butlerfoods.com

1-503-879-5005

Manufacturer of Soy Curls, a dry product made from the whole soybean.

METRIC CONVERSIONS AND EQUIVALENTS

METRIC CONVERSION FORMULAS

TO CONVERT	MULTIPLY
Ounces to grams	Ounces by 28.35
Pounds to kilograms	Pounds by .454
Teaspoons to milliliters	Teaspoons by 4.93
Tablespoons to milliliters	Tablespoons by 14.79
Fluid ounces to milliliters	Fluid ounces by 29.57
Cups to milliliters	Cups by 236.59
Cups to liters	Cups by .236
Pints to liters	Pints by .473
Quarts to liters	Quarts by .946
Gallons to liters	Gallons by 3.785
Inches to centimeters	Inches by 2.54

APPROXIMATE METRIC EQUIVALENTS

VOLUME

¼ teaspoon . . . . 1 milliliter	½ cup (4 fluid ounces) . . . . . .120 milliliters
½ teaspoon . . . . 2.5 milliliters	⅔ cup . . . . .160 milliliters
¾ teaspoon . . . . 4 milliliters	¾ cup . . . . .180 milliliters
1 teaspoon . . . . 5 milliliters	1 cup (8 fluid ounces) . . . . . . 240 milliliters
1¼ teaspoons . . . . 6 milliliters	1¼ cups . . . . 300 milliliters
1½ teaspoons . . . . 7.5 milliliters	1½ cups (12 fluid ounces) . . . . 360 milliliters
1¾ teaspoons . . . . 8.5 milliliters	1⅔ cups . . . . 400 milliliters
2 teaspoons . . . . 10 milliliters	2 cups (1 pint) . . . . 460 milliliters
1 tablespoon (½ fluid ounce) . . . .15 milliliters	3 cups . . . . 700 milliliters
2 tablespoons (1 fluid ounce) . . . 30 milliliters	4 cups (1 quart) . . . . 0.95 liter
¼ cup . . . . 60 milliliters	1 quart plus ¼ cup . . . . 1 liter
⅓ cup . . . . 80 milliliters	4 quarts (1 gallon) . . . . 3.8 liters

WEIGHT

¼ ounce . . . . .7 grams	3 ounces . . . . 85 grams
½ ounce . . . . 14 grams	4 ounces (¼ pound) . . . . .113 grams
¾ ounce . . . . 21 grams	5 ounces . . . . 142 grams
1 ounce . . . . 28 grams	6 ounces . . . . 170 grams
1¼ ounces . . . . 35 grams	7 ounces . . . . 198 grams
1½ ounces . . . . .42.5 grams	8 ounces (½ pound) . . . . 227 grams
1⅔ ounces . . . . 45 grams	16 ounces (1 pound) . . . . 454 grams
2 ounces . . . . 57 grams	35.25 ounces (2.2 pounds) . . . . . 1 kilogram

LENGTH

⅛ inch . . . . .3 millimeters	2½ inches . . . . 6 centimeters
¼ inch . . . . .6 millimeters	4 inches . . . . .10 centimeters
½ inch . . . . .1¼ centimeters	5 inches . . . . .13 centimeters
1 inch . . . . 2½ centimeters	6 inches . . . . .15¼ centimeters
2 inches . . . . 5 centimeters	12 inches (1 foot) . . . . 30 centimeters

OVEN TEMPERATURES

To convert Fahrenheit to Celsius, subtract 32 from Fahrenheit, multiply the result by 5, then divide by 9.

DESCRIPTION	FAHRENHEIT	CELSIUS	BRITISH GAS MARK
Very cool	200°	95°	0
Very cool	225°	110°	¼
Very cool	250°	120°	½
Cool	275°	135°	1
Cool	300°	150°	2
Warm	325°	165°	3
Moderate	350°	175°	4
Moderately hot	375°	190°	5
Fairly hot	400°	200°	6
Hot	425°	220°	7
Very hot	450°	230°	8
Very hot	475°	245°	9

COMMON INGREDIENTS AND THEIR APPROXIMATE EQUIVALENTS

1 cup uncooked white rice = 185 grams

1 cup all-purpose flour = 140 grams

1 stick butter (4 ounces • ½ cup • 8 tablespoons) = 110 grams

1 cup butter (8 ounces • 2 sticks • 16 tablespoons) = 220 grams

1 cup brown sugar, firmly packed = 225 grams

1 cup granulated sugar = 200 grams

Information compiled from a variety of sources, including *Recipes into Type* by Joan Whitman and Dolores Simon (Newton, MA: Biscuit Books, 2000); *The New Food Lover's Companion* by Sharon Tyler Herbst (Hauppauge, NY: Barron's, 1995); and *Rosemary Brown's Big Kitchen Instruction Book* (Kansas City, MO: Andrews McMeel, 1998).

INDEX

ABOUT THE AUTHOR

Julie Hasson is the author of eight cookbooks and has over twenty years of experience in the food industry, including serving as a private chef for celebrities and high-profile clients. Julie opened the original Babycakes Bakery in Los Angeles (a wholesale artisan bakery). She authored *Vegan Diner*, *150 Best Cupcake Recipes*, *The Complete Book of Pies*, *125 Best Cupcake Recipes*, *125 Best Chocolate Chip Recipes*, *125 Best Chocolate Recipes*, and *300 Best Chocolate Recipes*. Julie has contributed extensive articles and recipes to *Bon Appétit*, *Cooking Light*, *Vegetarian Times*, *VegNews*, and *Family Fun* magazines, and is also the host of the popular Internet cooking show *Everyday Dish*. Julie has been featured on numerous TV and radio shows across the country, including the Cooking Channel, *Better Portland*, *Good Day Oregon*, and Martha Stewart Living Radio. She was one of the hosts of the cooking show *15 and Done*, and was the Healthy Cooking Expert on *More Good Day Oregon*. Julie currently lives in Portland, Oregon, where she co-owns the food cart Native Bowl with her husband, Jay. She also runs Julie's Original, a company specializing in delicious gluten-free baking mixes.